· ON STRAWBERRY HILL ·

· ON STRAWBERRY HILL ·

THE TRANSCENDENT LOVE OF GIFFORD PINCHOT AND LAURA HOUGHTELING

PAULA IVASKA ROBBINS

FOREWORD BY CHAR MILLER

THE UNIVERSITY OF ALABAMA PRESS / TUSCALOOSA

The University of Alabama Press
Tuscaloosa, Alabama 35487-0380
uapress.ua.edu

Typeface: Warnock Pro

Cover portraits: Gifford Pinchot's graduation photograph from
Yale University; courtesy of the US Forest Service, Grey Towers
National Historic Site. Laura Houghteling in her youth; courtesy
of the US Forest Service, Grey Towers National Historic Site.
Title border: Unlisted Images / Fotosearch.com.
Cover design: Mary-Frances Burt / Burt&Burt

Library of Congress Cataloging-in-Publication Data

Names: Robbins, Paula I., author.
Title: On Strawberry Hill : the transcendent love of Gifford Pinchot and
Laura Houghteling / Paula Ivaska Robbins ; foreword by Char Miller.
Description: Tuscaloosa, Alabama : The University of Alabama Press,
[2017] | Includes bibliographical references.
Identifiers: LCCN 2016038221| ISBN 9780817358945 (pbk. : alk. paper) |
ISBN 9780817390945 (e book)
Subjects: LCSH: Pinchot, Gifford, 1865–1946. | Houghteling, Laura, died
1894. | Conservationists—United States—Biography. | United States—
History—19th century.
Classification: LCC S926.P56 R63 2017 | DDC 333.72092/273—dc23
LC record available at https://lccn.loc.gov/2016038221

In memory of the late James G. Bradley,
whom I never met.

· CONTENTS ·

• ILLUSTRATIONS •

· FOREWORD ·

"Did Gifford Pinchot really attend séances?" That's what a young entomologist asked me after a leadership training session with employees of the US Forest Service. Pinchot's controversial public career—he was the Forest Service's founding chief and later served two terms as the governor of Pennsylvania—had been one of the touch points of my talk. But my interlocutor was even more intrigued by his private life. In particular, she had heard a rumor that following the February 1894 death of Laura Houghteling, a woman with whom the then-26-year-old Pinchot was madly in love, he pined for her for the next twenty years. And sought to contact her through whatever spiritualist mediums were available. The rumors, I was happy to confirm, were not rumors, and then mentioned I was at that very moment reading *On Strawberry Hill*, the first book-length exploration of Gifford and Laura's fascinating love affair.

The twenty-first century might not understand theirs as a love affair; not for them the torrid consummation of unbridled passion. Children of considerable wealth, the pair were raised in the belief that one mark of their elevated status was self control, the capacity to rein in human appetites (sexual or otherwise). Cautious with their feelings, over the 18-month course of their deepening friendship and passionate engagement they managed an embrace or two and an embarrassed kiss. But they had no trouble imagining what might have been had Laura not suffered from tuberculosis; they pledged their troth with unfeigned intensity, a vibrant commitment made all the more so because of Laura's failing health. With her death on February 7, 1894, Pinchot donned a black suit of mourning that he would wear for the next two years; and in 1896, during a late-night vigil outside the Washington, DC, home where she had expired, he observed: "in God's sight, my Lady and I are husband and wife."

To track the narrative arc and emotional register of Laura and Gifford's relationship, Paula Ivaska Robbins has combed their diaries and read through their voluminous correspondence with family, friends, even nurses. Better, Robbins adds context to these literary leavings, establishing the historical landscape through which this besotted pair moved. They met in Asheville because, for Laura, its high ground and clear skies were reputed to be ideal for those who suffered from tuberculosis; it drew any number of well-heeled souls seeking respite, hoping to cleanse their lungs and heal their bodies. For Gifford, those very mountains and the vast forest that cloaked them offered his first formal job as a forester; he managed the woods that lay within George Washington Vanderbilt's sprawling Biltmore Estate, at that time the largest in the United States. Although fate may not have led Laura and Gifford to western North Carolina, their first meeting—given their physical proximity, as well as shared age and social class—was not really by chance, either.

Luck did not play a role in Laura's prognosis, either; there was no known cure for the dread disease known as consumption. But the couple faced this ravaging illness with an unflinching calm. This might seem puzzling, but Robbins assures that their behavior makes perfect sense. They were not the only Americans to embrace the teachings of Emanuel Swedenborg and other spiritual leaders who proclaimed the life-affirming connections between this world and the next. They were not alone in their fascination with the best-selling fiction of Elizabeth Stuart Phelps, whose *The Gates Ajar* (1868), *Beyond the Gates* (1883), and *The Gates Between* (1887) popularized the notion that there was a direct correspondence between heaven and earth. This soothing notion seemed tailor-made for a nation keening over the staggering losses suffered during the brutal Civil War, when nearly as many Americans died in three days at Gettysburg as were killed during the entire Vietnam War. Is it any wonder then that parents sought to reconnect with their lost sons, wives wished to reach out to deceased husbands, or children with their forever-absent fathers? Knowing that their time together was limited, Laura and Gifford vowed that theirs was an eternal bond; death could not separate that which would not, because it could not, perish.

In a very material sense, Gifford kept his part of the bargain, a lived reality that he recorded almost daily in his diary, that gave shape to whenever he delivered a speech and felt Laura's enveloping presence, and that he and his mother enacted whenever they visited spiritualists, mediums, and yogis in hopes of contacting his dearly departed. This very personal quest also had a profound impact on his professional career, as Robbins nicely details. In so doing, she gives us a more fully realized Gifford Pinchot: an ardent champion of forestry and a crusading conservationist, his work advancing the public good was fueled in part by his abiding memory of a young woman and the energizing love they shared.

—Char Miller

W. M. Keck Professor of Environmental Analysis at Pomona College and the author of *Gifford Pinchot and the Making of Modern Environmentalism* and *Seeking the Greatest Good: The Conservation Legacy of Gifford Pinchot*

· PREFACE ·

This is a story about two people and the place where they fell in love. The place was West Asheville, North Carolina, and knowing about its history—in the late nineteenth and early twentieth centuries—is essential to understanding how they came to know and love each other.

"I have . . . been a Governor every now and then, but I am a forester all the time."[1] In these words Gifford Pinchot emphasized what to him was the most important part of his varied career.

Although he served as the first head of an important federal agency, the US Forest Service, was active in national politics for more than a quarter-century, was a close friend and adviser of one president, played an important role in the downfall of another, and became a two-term governor of Pennsylvania, he never forgot his forestry roots and his concern for the conservation of America's natural resources.

Pinchot's biographer, Harold D. Pinkett, captures the importance of Pinchot's contribution to American society in the Introduction to his book. "But Pinchot was not just an ordinary forester. He was the first professionally trained American forester and the chief agent in the introduction of scientific forestry into the private and public woodlands of the United States."[2]

This small book is not a biography of Gifford Pinchot and his professional life, so ably documented by Char Miller in his *Gifford Pinchot and the Making of Modern Environmentalism*, but instead explores an interesting facet of his personal life that, until now, has not been broadly known or understood. By describing the nature of the relationship of Gifford Pinchot and Laura Houghteling, I delve into the practices and religious beliefs, no longer much studied, of many important and respected people of their time.

· ACKNOWLEDGMENTS ·

Many individuals were helpful to me in the making of this book. I first thought of writing about Gifford Pinchot and Laura Houghteling after reading Char Miller's *Gifford Pinchot and the Making of Modern Environmentalism.* The seed of the story was planted by Gene Hyde, Head of Special Collections and University Archivist of the Ramsey Library of the University of North Carolina at Asheville. He found and copied James G. Bradley's article from the digital library JSTOR, to which I did not then have access. He encouraged me to go ahead and build the structure around the article that had appeared in *Pennsylvania History.*

Most of my research for the book was conducted at the Buncombe County Pack Library North Carolina Room with the help of their wonderfully knowledgeable and helpful archivists.

Serendipitously, I sat across from a gentleman who overheard my conversation with one of the librarians and said to me, "It seems that we are both researching the same area." I later learned that his name was Ted Bugg, and he was a retired librarian from Nashville, Tennessee, who, as a hobby, researched the history of West Asheville. He grew up not far from the Strawberry Hill mansion in a house on Brevard Road built by J. D. Penland in 1903. He has been of great help to me and saved a lot of my time researching old deeds and making sure that I had not made any disastrous errors in the chapters dealing with Asheville history.

Several individuals knowledgeable about West Asheville history were most helpful in giving their time, references, and maps. They include Doug (Brotherhug) Barlow; Rick Russell, author of *Robert Henry: A Western Carolina Patriot*; Marcia Bromberg; Susan Roderick; and Karen Loughmiller, the head librarian at the West Asheville Branch Library and coordinator of the West Asheville History Project.

I am most grateful for the friendship, advice, and support of Drs. Martha and Gordon McKinney. Gordon, a historian and director emeritus of the Appalachian Center at Berea College, carefully read my manuscript and gave me an excellent tutorial on how to structure a book.

Susan Sunflower also read the manuscript and offered a number of good suggestions.

Ken Wolensky, President, and Dr. Karen Guenther, Business Manager, of the Pennsylvania Historical Association, which owns the copyright to James G. Bradley's article in *Pennsylvania History*, were most gracious and speedy in giving me permission to use the article as a basis for this book.

Rebecca Philpot, on the staff of Grey Towers National Historic Site, was very helpful and sent me the photos of Gifford, Laura, and Cornelia Bryce Pinchot, and of Grey Towers, as well as the papers of Doris Stillman regarding the books on Spiritualism that were in the Pinchots' library. Tim Barnwell brought the old photographs up to modern standards.

Just as I was polishing up my completed manuscript, I chanced to read a review of Marci Spencer's new book *Pisgah National Forest: A History*. Thus, I decided to add another chapter. Much of Chapter Twelve is based upon her excellent work, allowing me to finish my story on a forward-looking note.

Finally, I thank the staff of the University of Alabama Press for their fine work, especially, Elizabeth Motherwell, senior acquisitions editor for the natural sciences; Vanessa Rusch, managing editor; and L. Amanda Owens, copy editor.

· ON STRAWBERRY HILL ·

ASHEVILLE BECOMES A TOURIST DESTINATION

As early as 1837, before the Civil War and the coming of the railroads, Robert Henry and Reuben Deaver's hotel at the Sulphur Springs in West Asheville accommodated more than one hundred lodgers, many of them low-country planters and their families. These people would come to the mountains in the summer for a long stay to escape the heat and humidity of their homes. The spring's waters were said to benefit the skin and kidneys and act as a tonic.[1]

During his tour of the South, in July 1854, Frederick Law Olmsted visited the mountains and described the hotel in his book *A Journey in the Back Country*.[2] Little did he dream then that he would return to Asheville much later to work on one of the most important projects of his long career—at Biltmore Estate.

"Judge" Edward J. Aston, several times elected mayor of Asheville,[3] vigorously promoted Asheville as a health resort.[4] A wholesome, mild diet; outdoor exercise; and therapeutic rest in a suitable mild climate were at that time considered the

3

best treatment for phthisis (consumption). Aston contacted a number of prominent physicians, hoping to persuade them to move their practices to the city.

Dr. S. Westray Battle was one of the physicians who helped to build the city of Asheville as a health resort. Born to a prominent North Carolina family, he earned his bachelor's degree from the University of Virginia and received the degree of Doctor of Medicine in 1875 from Bellevue Hospital in New York City. At age 21, he was commissioned Assistant Surgeon in the Navy and served until 1884, establishing his residence in Asheville in 1885. He had studied government meteorological records and determined that the Asheville plateau had the driest atmosphere east of the Mississippi and, thus, was a suitable location for the cure of throat and pulmonary diseases and especially phthisis.[5]

Other physicians joined in promoting the area for health tourism, including Dr. Charles Minor, Dr. William Dunn, and Dr. Chase Ambler. Dr. Karl von Ruck, who had been an associate of Dr. Robert Koch, the German physician who first identified the cause of phthisis as the *Mycobacterium tuberculosis* in 1882, operated a sanitarium for patients with the disease on the old Sulphur Springs Hotel site from 1889 to 1896. He claimed that the clinical results of respiratory disease treatment in western North Carolina were unmatched elsewhere in the world. Dr. John Hay Williams, who came to Asheville in 1881 suffering from phthisis, claimed that he was cured by the climate. He remained to establish a practice treating others who had the disease.[6]

In October 1880, the Western Carolina Railroad was completed from Salisbury through Morganton, Marion, Old Fort, and

FIGURE 1. Carrier's Sulphur Springs Hotel before the 1890 wing addition; used by permission of the North Carolina Collection, Pack Memorial Public Library, Asheville, NC.

the Swannanoa Gap to the depot in the village of Best, on the east side of the French Broad River, making transportation available from the northeast. The Asheville-Spartanburg Railroad was completed in 1886, making access much easier from South Carolina. The railroad to Morristown, Tennessee, was finished in 1882, and the spur to Murphy, North Carolina, was opened in 1885.[7]

In 1886, the Charleston, Cincinnati and Chicago Railroad was incorporated, and construction began through Murphy to Cincinnati.[8] When that line was completed, tourists were able to come by train from the west via Louisville and locations in Ohio.[9] With easy access now available by rail, Asheville soon became a fashionable tourist resort for those who wished to partake of the local mineral springs and to enjoy the cooler climate and the beauty of the mountains.

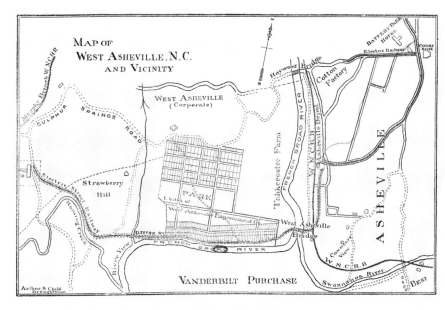

FIGURE 2. Map from *Compliments of West Asheville Improvement Company*; used by permission of the North Carolina Collection, Pack Memorial Public Library, Asheville, NC.

In 1885, Michigan lumber baron Edwin G. Carrier had stopped off in Asheville on his way to Florida to assess the business opportunities in western North Carolina. He must have found the possibilities enticing because, in 1887, Carrier built the Carrier Springs Hotel (later he changed its name to The Belmont) on the site of the original hotel at Sulphur Springs, which had burned down in 1862.[10] Carrier's hotel was considered ultra-modern and contained what was to be the first elevator in the South.

About 1890, Carrier also constructed a half-mile horseracing track on a flat area along the French Broad River to entertain his guests. It was fenced on all sides and had a large grandstand with seating. There he exercised his own stable of racehorses as well as those of others.[11]

On March 31, 1892, Carrier purchased, on behalf of a syndicate called The West Asheville Improvement Company, a tract of 1,200 acres, "lying around the Sulphur Springs, and reaching to the French Broad River."[12] The corporation planned a residential and business community that they named West Asheville and laid out streets and lots.

Carrier soon connected the area to the city of Asheville on the east side of the French Broad River by building a 250-foot steel-truss bridge just north of the junction of the Swannanoa and French Broad Rivers, connecting what is now Meadow Road with Amboy Road.[13]

Carrier also constructed a trolley route to connect the train depot on the east side of the French Broad River to carry his guests to the hotel at Sulphur Springs. The trolley ran across his bridge, along the west side of the French Broad River and the north side of Hominy Creek. Electric power for the trolley came from a low wooden dam across Hominy Creek. It was the first hydroelectric plant in western North Carolina and the first of its kind in the world to furnish power for a commercial streetcar. The West Asheville and Sulphur Springs Electric Railway began operation in August 1891.[14]

With the coming of the railroads and the increasing flow of tourists, more hotels were required. The 150-room Battery Park Hotel opened on July 26, 1886, situated on Battery Porter Hill, surrounded by a 25-acre park of ancient oaks and flower gardens. Among many other amenities, the hotel offered guests access to its stables, which held thirty to forty horses tended by fifteen to twenty stable hands.

In 1887, the 26-year-old George Washington Vanderbilt stayed at the Battery Park Hotel with his mother, hoping that the clear mountain air would help to cure her lingering malaria. During his stay, Vanderbilt hired horses from the stables and rode them around the area. The air was mild and invigorating, and he enjoyed the distant scenery and views of the mountain peaks. He found a spot with a beautiful view overlooking the French Broad River and decided that was where he wished to build a home.

In the spring of 1888, Vanderbilt commissioned his friend and attorney Charles McNamee to be his agent. McNamee quietly purchased numerous tracts of land surrounding the house site. Many of the purchases were from absentee owners. Vanderbilt's property would eventually comprise 125,000 acres on both sides of the French Broad River.

After McNamee had purchased sufficient land, Vanderbilt needed experts to assist him in deciding what to do with his property. He commissioned two of America's most prominent architects: Richard Morris Hunt, who had previously designed houses for various Vanderbilt family members, and landscape architect Frederick Law Olmsted, already well known for designing New York City's Central Park. Vanderbilt called his estate Biltmore, reflecting the family's Dutch origin. Hunt, who was an expert on the Beaux-Arts style, designed Vanderbilt's house using as models the architecture of several *Loire Valley* French Renaissance chateaux, including the Chateau de Blois.

It was not surprising that Olmsted would be disappointed at first with the land that Vanderbilt had purchased. The area had been logged over, removing most of the valuable trees except for oaks. The land consisted of barren hills with washed-out gullies, sedge fields, swamps, ditches, and a succession of worn-out farms with tumbledown houses in which their owners were starving. The soil in the area would require much improvement.

However, within fifty miles of Biltmore there were tall mountains with beautiful scenery and one of the finest deciduous forests in the world, with more biodiversity than almost any place in the nation. Because the Ice Age had pushed plants and animals south from more northerly climes, one could find trees in the high mountain coves that usually grew in areas as far north as Canada. At lower sheltered elevations one could also find plants found as far south as northern Florida. Thus, Olmsted recommended to Vanderbilt, "Such land in Europe would be made a forest; partly, if it belonged to a gentleman of large means, as a preserve for game, mainly with a view to crops of timber. That would be a suitable and dignified business for you to engage in; in the long run be probably a fair investment of capital and it would be of great value in the country to have a thoroughly well organized and systemically conducted attempt in forestry made on a large scale. My advice would be to make a small park into which to look from your house; make a small pleasure ground and garden, farm your river bottom chiefly to keep and fatten live stock with view to manure; and make the rest a forest, improving the existing woods and planting the old fields."[15]

Olmsted's suggestions for Biltmore required a trained forester to plan and manage the forest. Olmsted was an old friend of James Pinchot; thus, he must have been aware of James's son Gifford's training to become a forester, and he recommended that Vanderbilt hire the young man for the job.

• GIFFORD PINCHOT •

Gifford Pinchot was born in Simsbury, Connecticut, on August 11, 1865, in the home of his maternal grandfather, Amos R. Eno. As a child, Gifford spent his summers with his mother's family in Connecticut and the rest of his time in New York City, where his father, James Pinchot, was a wealthy wallpaper merchant. Because of his father's business interests abroad, the family traveled extensively in Europe during Gifford's childhood. As a result, he was conversant in German and French. He prepared for college at Phillips Exeter Academy and, in the fall of 1885, entered Yale College, where he took four years of French classes. He was active in evangelical Christian organizations, Bible-study classes, and volunteered at the Young Men's Christian Association (YMCA).[1]

James and his wife Mary were civic-minded supporters of the arts. James named his first son after the Hudson River School painter Sanford Gifford. Their circle of friends included many influential people in the Republican Party, such as General William Tecumseh Sherman. Among their friends was George Vanderbilt's choice of architect, Richard Morris

FIGURE 3. Grey Towers; courtesy of the US Forest Service, Grey Towers National Historic Site.

Hunt, who created a summer home called Grey Towers for them in Milford, Pennsylvania, where the family owned much property. Hunt designed Grey Towers to use local materials and to reflect the French heritage of the Pinchot family.

James's father, Cyril Constantine Désiré, was a Hugenot who had come to America in 1815 in search of political and religious freedom and first settled in Milford in 1818. For two decades after Grey Towers' completion in 1886, the Pinchots and their children enjoyed numerous summers there, entertaining guests for afternoon teas and dinner parties.

James, disturbed by destructive logging practices then prevalent in the United States, was familiar with foresters and their work in France and elsewhere in Europe. Just before Gifford, his eldest son, left for Yale, he asked him, "How would you like to be a forester?"[2] Gifford was intrigued; he loved the forest and had always enjoyed hiking, camping, and fishing. There was then no major in forestry at Yale or anywhere else in America. However, he was able to take related courses in meteorology, botany, geology, and astronomy. During his senior year, he went to Washington, DC, to consult with government officials regarding his plan to become a forester. Although they were discouraging about finding suitable employment, after graduation Gifford left for Europe to pursue his dream.

At the World Exposition in Paris in the summer of 1889, Pinchot saw an exhibit on water use and its relation to forests and obtained copies of some scientific treatises on forestry. He also met the renowned German forester Dietrich Brandis, who encouraged Gifford to enroll in the École Nationale Forestière in Nancy, France. There the young American studied silviculture, the art of producing and caring for forests, as well as economic aspects of forestry.[3] More importantly, he was able to walk in and observe the forests of Haye and Vandœuvres north of Nancy near Verdun that were managed by professional foresters. Here, the trees were harvested and seedlings were planted, thus reproduced like a crop. In the spring of 1890, Brandis arranged for Gifford to spend a month with an internationally famous Swiss forester who had charge of the ancient Sihlwald, a municipal forest of Zurich. It had been under systematic and profitable management for centuries. He was also able to tour other forests in France, Germany, and Switzerland.

It was in the forests of Haye, Vandœuvres, and Sihlwald that Gifford learned of a sustainable forestry that could retain forest resources for coming generations. This method would provide a middle ground between the wasteful clear-cutting or cherry-picking then so prevalent in America and the alternative of simply putting aside the forestlands as a forever untouchable park.

Impatient with the courses at Nancy, Gifford thirsted for practical American experience and dropped out after a year. Upon returning to the United States in 1890, he took a job surveying forestlands in Pennsylvania for Phelps, Dodge & Company.

Gifford then received an invitation to accompany Dr. Bernhard E. Fernow, a trained German forester who was Chief of the Forestry Division of the US Department of Agriculture, on a trip to inspect an area of timberland in Arkansas, where Gifford had his first chance to learn about the forests of the Mississippi Valley and to observe the tough southern lumberjacks. Fernow introduced Gifford to Dr. Charles Mohr, whom he assisted in a survey of mixed forests in northern Alabama.

In the spring of 1891 Gifford conducted another forest-inspection trip for Phelps, Dodge on the West Coast and in Canada. During this trip, he was able to see the Grand Canyon, eucalyptus trees growing in the San Gabriel Valley of California, the giant sequoias on the slopes of the Sierra Nevada, Douglas fir sawmills in Oregon and Washington, and the gigantic spruce in Vancouver's Stanley Park. Within six months of his return home to Pennsylvania, Gifford had seen forests in thirty-one states and in Canada and had actually examined them in nine states.

However, as he wrote in what he called his "personal story of how Forestry and Conservation came to America," "When I came home not a single acre of government, state, or private timberland was under systematic forest management anywhere on the most richly timbered of all continents. The

American people had no understanding either of what Forestry was or of the bitter need for it."[4]

On his way to Arkansas in February 1891, Gifford had already
visited Biltmore for a brief inspection trip and to meet Vanderbilt.[5] He wrote in his diary, "Vanderbilt's place just right for
forest management on a rather intensive plan. Hilly, but regen-
eration of conifer & deciduous both excellent and his house &
grounds will be absolutely gigantic."[6]

Gifford later wrote of Frederick Law Olmsted, whom he met
for the first time at Grey Towers while Olmsted had begun to
consult with George Vanderbilt,[7] "Mr. Olmsted was to me one
of the men of the century. He was a quiet-spoken little lame
man with a most magnificent head and one of the best minds
I have ever had the good luck to encounter. His knowledge
was far wider than his profession. He knew the territory of the
United States as few men knew it, and he was full of stories of
early days."

On December 6, 1891, Gifford called on Vanderbilt, and "it
was decided that I am to make his working plan for Biltmore."
On New Year's Eve, he went to Biltmore from New York with a
party including Hunt and Olmsted in Vanderbilt's private railroad car. The men talked about the feasibility of handling Vanderbilt's large property profitably. Gifford wrote in his diary,
"This traveling on private cars is something almost too good
for words."[8]

Gifford joined Vanderbilt's staff full-time on February 21,
1892. His contract called for an annual salary of $2,500 at a
time when the average worker earned about $500. He was to
create a plan for managing the forest at Biltmore and to pre-
pare an exhibit of this forest for the World's Columbian Expo-

sition that would be held in Chicago, opening on May 1, 1893. The exhibit was to demonstrate the practicality of scientific forestry in the United States and the need to preserve American forests for future generations.

Gifford attacked his mission with zeal. He wrote, "The more I know of the conditions the more thoroughly satisfied I am that if Biltmore forest is a success, I need not fear to undertake the management of any piece of forest land that I have seen in the United States."[9]

Gifford's first step was to compile data concerning the forest conditions, using a topographical survey already made that divided the property into squares of 500 feet. The purpose was to produce a constant annual yield and to improve the health of the forest. Large trees that were shading out younger and more vigorous ones were removed. Cattle were fenced and kept out of the forest, and fire-prevention methods were introduced. Fortunately, because of the construction of Vanderbilt's huge mansion and the accompanying Biltmore Village to house staff, there was a ready nearby use for all of the lumber produced.

In a letter to Brandis, Gifford conveyed his concerns that the forest would not provide immediate "money returns" for Vanderbilt's investment because "there is so much good lumber in the mountains, it is comparatively so cheap and our own is so distinctly poor, that we shall certainly be unable to do more than supply a little inferior sawn lumber and some fire wood for the local market and engage in the wood-distilling industry."[10]

In May 1892, Gifford made a quick trip to Europe to consult with several of his European mentors on the Biltmore Forest Exhibit that he was preparing for the Chicago World's Fair.[11]

Upon his return, he went to Chicago to see about arrangements there. When he returned to Biltmore, he spent some time surveying outlying forestland that Vanderbilt was considering for purchase and camping there in a tent overnight.

· NEIGHBORS ·

The railroad connections, the new hotels, the climate, the building of George Vanderbilt's mansion, and the perceived healthcare resources combined to make Asheville a magnet for developers and investors who fueled growth that would last for almost the next fifty years. In the late nineteenth century, Asheville was the fashionable place to be!

A group of wealthy Chicago businessmen were among those who were early attracted to Asheville to purchase land from the West Asheville Improvement Company to build summer or retirement homes for themselves. The company land extended from Carrier's Sulphur Springs hotel east to the French Broad River. The tract closest to the river was later loosely known as "Strawberry Hill." The group of businessmen included A. C. Bartlett; Charles Hutchinson; Martin A. Ryerson; William Rainey Harper, the first president of the University of Chicago; and William D. Houghteling.

Houghteling was a successful merchant and the vice-president of the Chicago Board of Trade and more than once had been president of the Chicago Lumber Exchange.[1] Sometime during the late 1880s, his daughter Laura had received a diagnosis of phthisis, or what was then called "consumption" in the upper-class society in which her family moved. Houghteling had learned of the salubrious qualities of Asheville's climate and the reputation of Dr. S. Westray Battle. As a result, Laura and other members of the family spent a lot of time in Asheville.[2]

Clearly, Houghteling believed that the Strawberry Hill neighborhood would be an ideal place to build a retirement home for himself and his family. He hoped that the climate and treatment by Dr. Battle would cure his daughter. Thus, in 1890, when he was seventy years old, Houghteling purchased a 12.75-acre site off the road from Asheville to Sulphur Springs, where some time earlier J. Adger Clark had built a small cottage on his then 100-acre Strawberry Hill Farm. Houghteling retained Clark's name of "Strawberry Hill" for his house.[3] (To avoid confusion, we will refer to "the Strawberry Hill neighborhood," the Houghteling's "Strawberry Hill property," and their "Strawberry Hill mansion.")

Houghteling commissioned the prominent Chicago architect Henry Ives Cobb to design a large mansion for his property. The house was 188 feet above the river on the point of land at the mouth of Hominy Creek. The house had six living rooms and ten bedchambers. Servants' quarters were in a separate building, and a stable had stalls for four horses.[4] By the end of 1891, the house was finished and members of the family had moved in.

Gifford Pinchot was twenty-six and Laura Houghteling was twenty-eight years old when they became neighbors.[5] Laura was already spending most of her time in Asheville when Gifford arrived at the end of January 1892. Gifford mentions in his diary that he "met Miss Houghteling after lunch" on October 17, 1891, when he came to Biltmore to look it over.[6] (Gifford had kept a detailed diary for some time and apparently did so for the rest of his life.)

Their first meeting after Gifford arrived to stay in Asheville may have occurred on February 7, 1892. It was the first time he called her "Laura." As he recorded it later in his diary, "She was coming up the long hill above the stream when I saw her first that day, and I think you waved your hand, my darling. Then we rode past the little white cabin to a knoll overlooking the FB. [French Broad River] and there I called you, 'Laura,' blushing very much meantime. (I felt so at least). You have told me since how surprised you were, but that you let it go because I seemed to think nothing of it."

Gifford and Laura already knew each other casually and had met at the same fashionable places every year. In 1886 and 1887, they both wintered in St. Augustine, Florida. In 1888, they saw each other at a wedding in San Francisco. In the summer of 1889, their paths crossed in Marblehead and Suffield, Massachusetts.

Laura, like other women of her social class probably "came out" at eighteen and was then expected to devote herself to being beautiful and charming in order to find a suitable husband. By her age of twenty-eight, she would have been expected to be married in a lavish ceremony. In 1892, she was close to an age when she would be considered "an old maid."

Pictures of Laura show a slender young woman with blond hair worn in a fashionable style on top of her head, light eyes, and a warm face. Sally Hewitt, a friend of the Pinchot family, called Laura "the most brilliant and beautiful woman" she had

FIGURE 4. Laura Houghteling; courtesy of the US Forest Service, Grey Towers National Historic Site.

ever seen. Ted Donnelly, a friend of Gifford's from Yale, wrote, "All the few lingering suspicions I had were dispelled the minute I saw Laura for she is certainly a queen."

Despite her beauty and intelligence, Laura had not married, probably because of her diagnosis of phthisis. Consumption carried a social stigma of being a disease of the slums and lower classes, as well as being caused by a hereditary weakness or familial predisposition.[7] When consumption attacked upper-class families, everyone was discreet. No one mentioned the name of Laura's illness, even in letters between family members and friends that discussed her condition.

Laura's doctor was handsome and charming, a brilliant conversationalist, a popular guest at dinner parties, and Asheville's favorite society doctor.[8] Unfortunately, nothing Dr. Battle ever did helped Laura or any of his other patients other than to give them and their loved ones hope.

Laura's room in the new house on Strawberry Hill must have been typical of sickrooms of the era. It probably faced south and had plenty of windows, with a wooden floor uncovered by carpets. The painted walls and furniture were easy to clean and disinfect. The bed was kept in the middle of the room for easy access by the attending nurse. The windows were kept open for good ventilation, and there may have been a sleeping porch.[9] "Those who contracted consumption were considered 'invalids.' The term was as much a social as a medical category, defining the responsibilities of the sick even as it freed them from fault. Invalids were obliged to seek cures and in turn were permitted, even expected, to modify social obligations in order to fulfill this special task. In the language of the day, invalids had a lifelong obligation to improve—with all the nuances of the phrase intended."[10]

At the time Laura moved to Strawberry Hill, there was no understanding of how diseases like phthisis spread or any effort to quarantine those who were affected. In addition, once invalids had moved to a healthful climate, they were encouraged to follow a regimen of outdoor exercise.[11] Laura thus soon joined the same social circle as Gifford, where the two frequently met.

Gifford was six feet two inches tall and sported a mustache that he kept all his adult life. His classmates at Yale voted him the most handsome man in his graduating class. As an eligible bachelor, he was soon invited to picnics, parties, and dances among the social circle of upper-class young people in the Asheville area.

FIGURE 5. Gifford Pinchot when he graduated from Yale; courtesy of
the US Forest Service, Grey Towers National Historic Site.

Laura's mother, Marcia Houghteling, invited the eligible
bachelor to join the family for dinner, and he often accepted.
He sheepishly wrote later of his experiences living in a house
left over from the former village of Best. "The first year at Biltmore I lived on the Estate in the Brick House, which was kept
open for George's [Vanderbilt] convenience and mine. While I
was a fair camp cook, I was perfectly green at Housekeeping.
But when the bill came in for sixteen dozen eggs and a gallon
of cream in one week, even I could understand that 192 eggs
in seven days exceeded the capacity for eggs of two men and
one ancient colored cook. Just how many of Martha's children
and grandchildren and children-in-law were being fed on the

food we were supposed to eat I never learned—but certainly plenty."[12]

Mrs. Houghteling must have queried him about his work, and he would have been eager to explain. As he later wrote in *Breaking New Ground*, his autobiography, he might have answered her,

> Forestry is Tree Farming. Forestry is handling trees so that one crop follows another. To grow trees as a crop is Forestry.
>
> Trees may be grown as a crop just as corn may be grown as a crop. The farmer gets crop after crop of corn, oats, wheat, cotton, tobacco, and hay from his farm. The forester gets crop after crop of logs, cordwood, shingles, poles, or railroad ties from his forest, and even some return from regulated grazing.
>
> Because the plants he grows ripen in a single season, the farmer usually gets a crop every year from the land he farms. The forester, because the plants he grows—his trees—mature only after many seasons, may get his crop from the same acre only once in thirty or fifty or a hundred years, or even longer.
>
> Good Forestry, in addition to lumber, firewood, and other produce, yields such services as regulation of stream flow, protection against erosion, and some influence on climate.
>
> Each succeeding crop of trees may come up, like each succeeding crop of hay, either from seed sown by the preceding generation or by sprouts from the old roots. Or young trees may have to be planted, just as each crop of tobacco has to be set out.
>
> Different kinds of trees must be handled in different ways.[13]

Although he was busy with his work, Gifford was often able to meet Laura for sedate horseback rides along the French Broad River on weekends. We can imagine her seated sidesad-

FIGURE 6. View of the French Broad River from Strawberry Hill; used by permission of the North Carolina Collection, Pack Memorial Public Library, Asheville, NC.

dle on her horse and dressed in a hat and appropriately long riding skirt. During these outings, he would likely point out the names of the important native trees along their path and their value and use: chestnut, white pine, sugar maple, tulip or yellow poplar, and white, red, and chestnut oak, as well as many others. From their conversations, she began to understand and support his missionary zeal for what he was doing.

Laura's health fluctuated and on her bad days Gifford would come to visit her at home. One can imagine a scene such as this upon Gifford's return from his travels in August 1892: Laura would be seated in a wicker chaise lounge on the broad veranda shaded by the leaves of a large chestnut tree, which did little to mitigate the sultry August air. Reclining in her perch next to the matching wicker sewing table, she could barely glimpse the French Broad River glimmering below the hill, but she was able to see the rolling countryside on the other side, with forests and mountains in the distance.

In between glances at the stitches of her embroidery, Laura's eyes concentrated on the crude path that had been trod at the edge of the broad lawn by horse's hooves over the past months from the river below to the barn behind the house.

It is likely that Gifford was able to cross the French Broad River by use of a simple ferry. Local lore has it that the ferry was used during the construction of Biltmore to bring dynamite used to excavate the foundation from a safe storage place along the west side of the French Broad River. The curious stone storage place can still be seen along the greenway from Hominy Creek Park to Carrier Park. The ferry was also used to transport milk from dairy farms on the west side for the construction workers before the Biltmore dairy was built.[14]

Soon, Gifford's tall slender figure on horseback appeared at the foot of the path, and Laura waved as the horse passed the end of the veranda on the way to the barn behind the house, where she knew the horse would be stabled and the rider would change from his riding breeches to more suitable attire. She was glad that she had worn her new white dimity frock.

"Julia, Mr. Pinchot is here," she called. "Please bring a pitcher of sweet tea. He'll certainly be thirsty after his ride."

After a few minutes, her nurse and companion Julia Sullivan would return with a tray carrying a tall pitcher and three glasses, followed by Gifford Pinchot, handsome and mustachioed. Their conversation would be formal, addressing each other as Mr. and Miss.

"Do sit down, Mr. Pinchot. How was your trip to Europe and then Chicago? I hope that the plans for the Fair are progressing well. Won't you have some tea?" Laura would gesture to the large wicker wing chair across from her while Miss Sullivan would fill two tall glasses for Laura and her guest before filling one for herself.

After taking a long draught, Gifford might say, "That was refreshing; it's such a hot day. But you look quite fresh, despite the heat, Miss Houghteling. I hope you are feeling well."

"Yes, Mr. Pinchot, I am feeling much better. I've actually gained a pound. Mother and I went in the fiacre yesterday to see Dr. Battle, and he always makes me feel much better just by seeing him. He is such a courtly gentleman! Tall and straight as a ramrod from his years in the Navy. There's always a carnation or rose boutonnière in his white cotton coat as well as in the lapel of his white flannel suit jacket, and he wears a black silk sash over it. When we come in, he bows low to greet us."[15]

"Dr. Battle told us more about the terrible fire on the night of the 24th at Dr. Van Ruck's Belmont Hotel. As you may know, the fire began about 11:30 that night, and totally destroyed all three floors. Many of the guests staying in the top floor had to jump to the second-floor veranda." Dr. Van Ruck carried his wife, who was ill, to safety. Fortunately, all 138 guests staying in the hotel survived. One woman lost her child for several hours in all the confusion, but, fortunately, he was finally reunited with his frantic mother.[16]

"I've invited the Hawkins family from Raleigh to stay here for several days until they can find transportation home. There's plenty of room for them, with just Julia and Mother and me here."[17]

Soon Gifford and Laura were in love. In addition to their good looks and their similar wealthy family backgrounds, there were inner qualities that drew Gifford and Laura together. Gifford was a crusader. Instead of a career making money and expanding the family fortune, which his maternal grandfather, Amos R. Eno, would have preferred,[18] he devoted his life to public service in altruistic causes, particularly conservation.

Much less information can be found about Laura but letters about her and what Gifford wrote in his diaries about her indicate that she had a special inner beauty.

Nurse Julia wrote in a letter to Gifford, "I think in everybody's life there is a turning point and it came to me when I went away with dear Miss Laura. I had read a great deal of noble natures and beautiful minds but I thought it never existed in everyday life because I had never encountered one. Miss Laura taught me so much different. I learned how to be good and true and how to live for other people. Mr. Pinchot, I could never tell of the good she did me. She was so unselfish. . . . If there is any good in me, I have her to thank for it. She made me by her own example, considerate to others and also to be just in all things. . . . She had the happy faculty of making all that came in contact with her, love her and she was never too proud to talk to people less fortunate than herself."

Laura's name is mentioned in *Asheville and Vicinity: A Handbook of Information* in the section about Asheville Mission Hospital. "Through the generous offer of Miss Laura Houghteling in 1891, of $1500 as a contribution to a new building, the managers were enabled to start a financial campaign sufficiently successful to justify the erection of a new building, which was ready for occupation December 18, 1892."[19]

One afternoon when Mrs. Houghteling had left the house to visit friends, Gifford and Laura had their first passionate embrace. Julia Sullivan was their chaperone that day, but Laura had sent her from the parlor to bring Gifford some tea. When she returned, she discovered Gifford and Laura in a small settee by the fireplace with Gifford holding Laura in his arms, both oblivious of Julia's presence. In a letter to Gifford, a year after Laura's death, Julia wrote, "I was so frightened I came near dropping the tray and came very near saying 'Excuse me' or something like that. She told me all about it that night after we went upstairs to bed and she said that if I had ever said 'excuse me' she would never have forgiven me."

This first embrace was a magical moment for Laura. Julia observed, "I shall never forget how happy she seemed. She asked me then if I thought she had better tell her mother and I told her 'yes' and the next day she did. From that time on she wanted to get well so badly. She would stay in bed and rest and then imagine that rest was all she wanted to make her well."

In the spring of 1893, Gifford and Laura began telling their friends and family about their feelings for each other, although he had written to some of his Yale friends the previous October.[20] In a letter to his mother, Gifford wrote, "Miss Houghteling . . . is in great repute with all of us. I have seldom met so sane and straightforward a girl or one with so little foolishness about her. We discuss the state of the universe from time to time and arrange its details and have a very jolly time together."

In a conversation with a mutual friend, Laura described her feelings for Gifford with one succinct phrase, "Mr. Pinchot—he is just glorious!"

The Chicago World's Fair opened on May 1, 1893. Gifford wrote, "The Biltmore Forest Exhibit at Chicago was, so far as I know, the first exhibit of practical Forestry ever made in the United States. It showed by greatly enlarged photographs what the forest was like, and what had already been done to improve it while making it pay."[21] Gifford wrote and distributed a free pamphlet describing the work, which was picked up by visitors and especially by newspapers. Laura probably went home to Chicago to view the exhibit and to see Gifford there.

Gifford notes in his diary for September 11 that he had gone to Sunday school and "after lunch rode over and called on Laura Houghteling and then back here for supper." [22]

By December, they had decided to marry and apparently Gifford asked his family for their support. This caused consternation with his parents and siblings. They knew that Laura was dying. Although they could never discuss this with Gifford, who was convinced that she would recover and that she already was getting better, they did debate her illness and the proposed marriage amongst themselves. Gifford's sister Nettie championed Gifford's cause. She wrote to their mother, Mary Pinchot, "It's rather hard luck that Miss Houghteling has had health problems, but there is nothing like happiness to cure. . . . I think she must be delightful and certainly everyone says she is most charming and clever and if she looks like Mrs. Canfield (Laura's sister) there's little left to wish. . . . It's a blessing to see him so entirely recovered from the melancholy[23] young person of last summer and I must say that I feel as if Laura Houghteling had let us back the old cheery Gifford. . . . It is comforting to hear all the lovely things which everyone says about her. . . . Dear old Gifford, he deserves to be happy, doesn't he? I am still in a wild state of excitement about it all and I can't keep my mind on Christmas presents at all!"

By New Year's 1894, Gifford's parents gave their support, and Gifford wrote to his father: "I thank you from my heart."

CONSUMPTION BECOMES TUBERCULOSIS

I n the nineteenth century, consumption was the leading cause of death in the United States.[1] "Tuberculosis was a cunning disease," writes Thomas Goetz, "coming on slowly, almost casually. At first it seemed innocuous, beginning with a cough; a cold, perhaps, or a touch of bad air. But then that cough turned malevolent, becoming stronger and more painful and extracting blood with each spasm. Then the appetite would go, replaced by fatigue, a deep dullness that would pull the sufferers into lethargy. Eventually, bodies would begin to wither and dissipate from within. For most consumptives, this played out over months and years. Even when the end seemed imminent, it was as if the consumptives could not muster the energy to die—until, finally, they did."[2]

The ancient Greeks were the first to label the symptoms of the disease as "phthisis" (literally "wasting" or "consumption"), in which the body was literally consumed by the disease.[3]

In 1882, the German physician and scientist Robert Koch identified the tubercle bacillus, *Mycobacterium tuberculosis*.

Koch soon realized the implications of his findings: Tuberculosis was an infectious disease that could be diagnosed by the presence and the growth and multiplication of bacilli. Tuberculosis could be differentiated from other diseases such as pneumonia and could be recognized as one common disease whether it was the lungs, intestines, or skeleton that was infected. Because tuberculosis usually began in the respiratory tract, it was apparent that the bacilli were spread through the air.[4]

The idea of germs, *little animalcules*, causing disease was still radical and then outside the bounds of traditional medicine. However, in 1854, physician John Snow deduced that the contaminated Broad Street pump had caused the cholera epidemic in London.

Koch had been inspired by the work of Louis Pasteur, who had demonstrated that the microorganisms described by the inventor of the microscope, the Dutchman Antonie van Leeuwenhoek, were responsible for both normal and abnormal fermentation. Pasteur's work also inspired Joseph Lister of Edinburgh to develop antisepsis, "the most important single surgical advance of the past 200 years."[5]

Soon, Koch's discoveries led to a change in terminology: *consumption* was replaced by *tuberculosis*. They also led, ultimately, to the growing prestige of the medical profession and confidence that the scientific method would lead to the conquest of communicable diseases.[6] The public was cautioned to avoid "promiscuous spitting" because the major source of transmission was the sputum from the cough of an infected person. Healthy people could also avoid infection if they were careful to eat a wholesome diet, get fresh air and exercise, and keep clean.

At the Tenth International Congress of Medicine in Berlin in 1900, Koch "announced that he had discovered a substance that could 'in some cases' protect against tuberculosis and even 'under certain circumstances' cure the disease."[7] The front page of the *New York Times* of January 7, 1891, featured a story about Robert Koch's announcement of the discovery of tuberculin, a substance derived from tubercle bacilli, which he thought was capable of arresting bacterial development in vitro and in animals. This news gave rise to tremendous hope throughout the world, which was soon replaced by disillusionment when the product turned out to be an ineffective therapeutic agent. However, tuberculin caused an immune reaction and later proved to be a valuable diagnostic tool.[8]

In 1921, Benjamin Weill-Hallé and Raymond Turpin administered the first live-attenuated tuberculosis vaccine to a human at the Charité hospital in Paris. This oral Bacille Calmette-Guérin vaccine is still the standard of preventive care, yet it has unpredictable results and gives only some protection to young children against the most severe forms of the disease. In the past century, no one has figured out how to make a better vaccine.[9]

An effective treatment for tuberculosis was finally achieved in the 1940's by Selman Waksman and a graduate student, Albert Schatz, at Rutgers University. Waksman received a Nobel Prize for the discovery of streptomycin, the first antibiotic effective in treating tuberculosis. After World War II, doctors began the use of the "Triple Therapy" of streptomycin, PAS (para-aminosalicylic acid), and isoniazid, but an end to tuberculosis still eludes medical science today. Treatment of multiple drug–resistant tuberculosis remains a difficult problem requiring lengthy treatment with toxic drugs.

• WASHINGTON, DC •

By December 1893, the Houghtelings realized that Laura's treatment in Asheville was not working, and that month they moved her to Washington, DC, to try a new team of doctors. They may have been physicians experimenting with the use of tuberculin or some similar substance.

According to Julia Sullivan, "she cried very bitterly when she bid her father, mother, and house goodbye" and that she told her room, "Goodbye my pretty room, perhaps I shall never see you again, but if I do I will be a healthy woman."

Laura stayed with her uncle, Senator Frank Stockbridge of Michigan, in his large mansion that dominated the corner of Connecticut Avenue and R Street, N.W. It looked like an Italian Palazzo constructed from red brick and salmon-colored limestone, decorated on the outside with cornices, balustrades, arches, and Palladian windows. Inside, there were bay windows looking out, marbled fireplaces, hand-carved woodwork, mosaic and parquet floors, and a grand staircase climbing to the fourth floor.

In the same month that Laura moved to Washington, Gifford moved to New York City, where he lived with his par-

FIGURE 7. Laura Houghteling; courtesy of the US Forest Service, Grey Towers National Historic Site.

ents at Number Two, Gramercy Park. Gifford opened an office on Fourth Avenue at 22nd Street in New York City. The sign on the door read "Consulting Forester." Gifford wrote: "My arrangement with George Vanderbilt left me free to take on additional work." "I found myself growing impatient for fresh fields and pastures new." "I was kept busy as a bee."[1]

Whenever he could, he took the train to Washington to be with Laura,[2] staying two blocks away from Senator Stockbridge's house at Number Two, Dupont Circle, the home of his sister Nettie and her English diplomat husband, Lord

Alan Johnstone. Three days after she moved in with her Uncle Frank, Laura came to visit Gifford at Nettie's. Because of her frailty, he carried her in his arms up the stairs, a tender moment that Laura treasured.

As Laura's condition worsened, Mary Pinchot decided that she had better come to Washington to see Laura and her son. This was a big event for Laura, and she tried to make a good impression. Julia notes, "I think it was on Sunday, Dec. 1st, that your mother came to call on Miss Laura. She went down to see her and she wanted to appear so well to her. She told me on no account to bring her any medicine while your mother was in the house. . . . Miss Laura put on her red dress to go down to see her. You remember the dress, do you not? She had her picture taken in it. How she did love that tea gown and how lovely she looked in it."

Three days later, Laura went to bed and never walked again. Because, at first, she was too modest to let Gifford into her bedroom, he would read to her from an adjoining sitting room. Soon, however, with Julia's urging, she relented and Gifford would sit by her bedside.

Sometime in early January 1894, Laura's doctors told her there was no hope. Her reaction was an example of the nobility that so impressed Julia. She was more worried about those around her than about herself. Julia wrote, "When Dr. Johnson came in afterwards and told her what her fate was to be, she felt so sorry for him to think that he had to tell her. And I stood by her bed and felt as if my heart was breaking. She was so calm and collected. And she told me she expected it. And then she said 'Oh, Julia, how can I tell Gifford?' She said she knew you would not believe it, but it had to be. She had felt it for a long time."

Laura was right about Gifford. He never did believe it, before or after her death. During Laura's last days, Gifford's family agonized about him, worrying about how he would survive this ordeal, but throughout it all he never lost his hope, his courage, or his self-control. Nettie wrote to their mother: "Poor Gifford looks terribly white and worn and I fancy has not slept at all. There seems nothing one can do for him as he doesn't talk of it and we don't like to ask him questions as it makes it harder for him to keep his self-control. I only hope that he does not think us unsympathetic for indeed we think and talk of nothing else, and dream of him and of poor Laura all night long. He is very brave, as of course, he would always be. . . . I really have not known what to do about Gifford and so far have told no one. What are you going to do?"

Gifford tried to reassure his family. In a letter to his father, James Pinchot, full of hope and optimism and hinting at the posthumous relationship that was to come, he wrote: "While there is no real cause for encouragement, as I greatly fear, still I am feeling more hopeful about her. . . . It seems as though it must come out as we hope, although both Laura and I have faced the other and talked it fully over and are not afraid because we know it can be nothing more than a temporary separation, short for her, however long it may be for me. She is so splendidly brave about it, so strong and unselfish, and we feel so strongly what I have just said, that it is all much less terrible than it must seem to you and indeed to anyone but ourselves. I have not been able to tell this to anyone as yet, so I am glad to write it and especially to have you and Mamee [his mother] know just how we feel for I am sure you will sympathize with us entirely."

Apparently, Gifford and Laura already had decided they would be together after her death. They had discussed it and they knew in advance just how it would happen.

On February 5, 1894, Laura spoke her last words, still thinking of others instead of herself. Julia wrote to Gifford: "And to think her last conscious words were to me and even then to think of someone else's good. Do you want to know what they were? She could hardly speak and I had to bend close to her to hear what she said. It was 'Julia dear, I want you to go out this afternoon and have a good time. You've been so much in the house of late.' I kissed her hand and she smiled at me and then turned her head and commenced to say a little prayer but she could not finish it. It died away and that was the last conscious thing she said. I can see it all so plainly. It lives in my memory as fresh as if it were yesterday."

Two days later at 8:45 P.M., Thursday, February 7, 1894, Laura died.

Laura Houghteling was physically beautiful, but it was the beauty of her inner spirit that made this love story possible. As Nurse Julia wrote, Laura was "an angel of goodness." After her death, she became Gifford's angel, his guide and inspiration.

Laura's obituary in the *Asheville Daily Citizen* of February 9, 1894, indicates what local residents thought of her.

> Dr. S. Westray Battle has received a telegram bearing the sad intelligence that Miss Laura Houghteling, daughter of William D. and Marcia E. Houghteling, died yesterday at the house of Senator Stockbridge in Washington City. Heart disease was the cause of Miss Houghteling's death.

Miss Houghteling was well known in Asheville in and near which city she has lived for several years. She was a handsome young lady and lovely in every trait of character. Many people will never forget the noble work she did in aiding occupants of the Belmont Hotel when they were driven from the building on the night of the memorable Belmont Fire. The many friends of the highly esteemed lady will hear of her death with the keenest sorrow.

Miss Houghteling's remains will be interred at Chicago.

Telegraphed in New York, Mary Pinchot wrote in her diary, "Laura died today. Poor Gifford." Mary McCadden, a family friend and Gifford's childhood nanny, wrote to Gifford's brother Amos, "When Miss Laura died, I thought my very heart would break." A college friend from Yale wrote, "It is something more precious than anything else in the world just to have loved a noble woman."

The family feared that Laura's death might devastate Gifford. Nettie wrote to Amos, "Dearest Toots, the family has no doubt let you know that Laura died last night. Gifford came at half past nine to tell us. He is taking his sorrow most wonderfully. He is so brave and quiet about it, but I think he will never be the same cheery old Gifford again. . . . Gifford has been at [Laura's Uncle Frank's] day and night since Monday and looks badly as he has had no sleep. But I don't think he will break down."

Mary Pinchot told Amos, "I have no doubt that in the end it will all come out right. Things always do when faith and hope with high mind lead the way. Gifford has all of these, though for the moment they seem to be almost veiled by his sorrow. All does not always come out as we wish, but there is no doubt that since God so let it be, that it is right. I believe that Gifford has a high and noble mission to fulfill and I believe that he will do it—but I don't want to see him narrowing himself down to one thought. It is not right in this world to live in the past or with the dead."

Gifford continued to carry on with the same calm courage that he had shown during Laura's illness. The day after her death, he travelled with the Houghtelings to Chicago to attend her memorial service in the Chapel at Graceland Cemetery. Mrs. Houghteling wrote, "Those nearest and dearest were gathered, and triumphant songs were sung and the last that love could do was done."

Graceland Cemetery remains a beautiful place, beautifully maintained. Laura's grave lies on a knoll under a tree. On her stone is "Laura Houghteling" and nothing else, not even dates. The cemetery records omit her date of birth and give her age as twenty-four, even though Gifford's notes record that she actually was twenty-eight. Perhaps high society considered it an embarrassment to be that old and still unmarried.

Gifford apparently had no interest in her grave, as he never mentioned returning to the site. He knew that she was not really there.

• TRANSCENDENT LOVE •

On March 18, 1894, thirty-eight days after Laura's death, a startling passage appears in Gifford's diary. "My lady is very near." On April 3, he felt that she had arrived: "My Darling is with me and I know it already." From then on, he felt her presence continuously. "A wonderful day with my Dearest clearly with me" (October 31); and "My Lady spoke to me tonight" (December 8).

For twenty years, Gifford secretly wrote about Laura and their ongoing relationship in his private diaries as if she were a living presence who never had left him. She spoke to him, traveled with him, read books with him, advised him, and inspired him. Typical entries are: "My lady has told me beautiful things" (April 16, 1894); "I know that she is always here" (October 4, 1894); and "Tonight my Dearest spoke to me, saying she wants to be with me as much as I want to be with her" (January 1, 1895).

There is no grief in this relationship. His diaries are filled with entries describing his joy at still being with Laura. "A wonderful happy day, full of her presence and peace" (April 15,

1894); and "My lady is so clearly with me that I cannot say how deeply happy and grateful I am" (December 13, 1894).

Gifford apparently believed that Laura had come back to him, just as they had planned. Defying human reason, Gifford and Laura seemed to have reunited in some mysterious way. There is no sorrow in his diaries about Laura and no mention of death; their relationship was warm and joyous. Instead, the diaries are full of love, happiness, and peace. "A happy day with my Lady" (February 22, 1896). "A peaceful, beautiful day with my Lady" (February 23, 1896). "I was blessed with a wonderful nearness of my Dearest in the train to Frankfurt. I could hardly help expecting to see her with my own eyes" (May 16, 1895). "A wonderful day. I dreamed of my Dearest last night and today she has been beautifully near. I can not thank our Father in Heaven enough" (June 16, 1899).

After Laura died, Gifford often passed by her uncle Frank's house, her last home. It became a hallowed place for Gifford, who called it "our house." Frank unexpectedly died three months after Laura, and her relatives moved away. For years Gifford would visit "our house" late at night, apparently standing outside in the shadows in a meditative state believing that Laura was with him. Three years after her death, he wrote in his diary, "We went to our house together late tonight" (January 1897) and then in the following year, "To our house with my Laura" (April 1988).

Gifford's secrecy about Laura included a code that he used in his diaries to indicate whether or not he had felt Laura's presence on a particular day. On the surface, the coded entries appear to describe the weather or what kind of day he had. On days that he felt Laura was with him, he would write, "a bright day" or "a clear day." If he was having difficulty reaching her but knew that she was near, his usual entry was "not a clear day." Sometimes there were bleak days when he could not find Laura at all and the code described his pain: "a dull, dead day"; "a blind day"; "a lifeless, useless day "; "I'm going blind."

Gifford used the code inconsistently in writing about Laura, openly one day and in code the next. Because no reader possibly could be misled by these entries, it is part of the mystery why he wrote code at all.

The one person he did share his secret with was Marcia Houghteling, Laura's mother. He trusted and loved her and knew she would understand. She felt the same about Gifford.[1] Gifford's diaries imply that Mrs. Houghteling also believed that Laura had not really died and that she joined Gifford in his effort to reunite with her. She and Gifford would sit together in Laura's room at Strawberry Hill looking at her things and talking late into the night.

During those twenty years that he communed with Laura, Gifford did not marry, much to the disappointment of his parents. They hoped that Gifford, as the first-born son and their most successful offspring, would marry and father another generation of the Pinchot family.

Newspaper gossip columnists in Washington considered this wealthy, handsome, and successful man as "the most eligible bachelor in the city." Yet he seemed married to his work.[2]

In many ways, Gifford *was* married to his work. Had he enjoyed a conventional marriage with children, it would have been unlikely and perhaps impossible for him to accomplish all that he had during the twenty years after Laura's death, especially the time spent traveling by rail, sea, and horseback.

Their surreptitious relationship provided the personal support and psychological sustenance that marriage would have brought him, without the time-consuming physical baggage.

Gifford lived his inner life with Laura in secrecy. Some of his friends and colleagues would have been amazed and perhaps shocked to know that he believed that Laura was still with him. How could the nation's leading proponent of the use of scientific forestry also believe in communication after death?

The story of their love had never been told until the late James G. Bradley found the parts of his diary that were suppressed by Gifford's family and ignored by other scholars. After Gifford's death in 1946, his family donated his papers and diaries to the Library of Congress, but withheld key documents about Laura, including all correspondence between her and Gifford and Gifford's diary for 1893, the year of their courtship. They have disappeared or are lost, hidden, or destroyed.

• SPIRITUALISM •

What did Gifford really mean when he wrote in his diary that he and Laura were still together? How was it possible for him to maintain a twenty-year relationship with someone who was dead? Was he seeing ghosts, hallucinating, or living a fantasy? Had grief made him mentally unstable? For some, Gifford's diary entries might indicate that he was a grief-stricken and troubled soul, living in a fantasy world.

Instead, the twenty years after Laura's death encompassed Gifford's greatest and most celebrated accomplishments. According to historian Thomas R. Wellock, "The profession of forestry came of age during the Progressive Era. In no small part this was due to the efforts and financial support of Gifford Pinchot."[1]

The following chapters will provide an outline of Gifford's many accomplishments during the twenty years that he communicated with Laura, from soon after her death in 1894 until the early summer of 1914.

But why, many would still ask, would one of the most prominent Progressive Era advocates of the practical use of modern science in forestry in his professional life secretly hold to the metaphysical practice of Spiritualism in his personal life?

This is the heart of the mystery of the relationship of Gifford and Laura during those twenty years. Fear that this story would be interpreted negatively and used to show that Gifford was flawed in some way is probably the reason his family and admirers suppressed the diary of that time period for so many years.

Gifford was a regular churchgoer and a believing Christian. He had been active in the YMCA during his years at Yale and was selected deacon for the class of 1889. He considered becoming a minister or serving in the settlement house movement.[2] In his diary, he often mentions that he had heard the Rev. Dr. Charles Henry Parkhurst preach at the Madison Square Presbyterian Church in New York City.

The editor of Gifford's journal, Harold K. Steen, wrote, "Perhaps the best explanation [of the mystery of Gifford and Laura's communication after her death] is the theory that Pinchot was a practitioner of Spiritualism, and there is ample evidence to support this view."[3]

Gifford attended the Church of the Holy City, the National Swedenborgian Church on Dupont Circle in Washington, DC.[4]

The website of the Swedenborgian Church of North America lists the church's beliefs, including: "People are essentially spirits clothed with material bodies. At death, the material body is laid aside and the person continues to live on in the world of spirit choosing a heavenly life or a hellish one, based on the quality of life choices made here."[5]

The original church organization was based on the work of Emanuel Swedenborg (1688–1772), a Swedish scientist and theologian who was considered a forerunner of Spiritualism. "He was an authority on metallurgy, an astronomer, a zoologist, anatomist, physicist, financier, and a profound biblical scholar."[6]

The established Christian belief was that on a person's death, his soul went to Heaven or Hell, or—as Catholics believe—to Purgatory. By contrast, Swedenborg described the afterlife as being very similar to this life . . . and that communication between the two worlds was possible.[7]

The library at Grey Towers held a large collection of books on Spiritualism, according to Doris Spillman of Columbia University, who cataloged them in her "Spirit: Notes on references to spiritualism in books in Grey Towers Library." One particular book about Swedenborg apparently belonged to James Pinchot. The inscription reads, "James W. Pinchot, Esq. from his friend John Bigelow."[8] Bigelow wrote about his experience of reading Swedenborg's works.

The solution to the mystery of Gifford and Laura's relationship is revealed in one simple diary entry: "Laura is one with God" (August 8, 1898). The relationship between Gifford and Laura after her death was spiritual. It was a private religious experience emanating from his and Laura's understanding of God. What those trying to protect Gifford's reputation did not understand was that Gifford did not think that he was seeing or hearing a physical or ghostly presence, but rather a spiritual one. He communicated with her in his mind and through his spiritual consciousness of God. Gifford did not use a medium as a go-between, as many Spiritualists did.

"Tonight I saw my Lady in my Mind and I thank God for it" (April 28, 1895). "A deeper consciousness of my Dearest and her care for me" (January 13, 1897).

When Laura was with him, God was with him. When he felt close to God, he felt close to Laura. Laura's presence was God's presence. In his mind, he and Laura were united in God. "My Lady and I are in the sight of God" (August 2, 1894). "It has been a marvelous day. My Dearest was with me this morning as I could hardly have believed possible, even after all of God's Goodness" (January 28, 1895). "A wonderful, wonderful day. Thank God for the light" (June 11, 1902).

Laura was that light. She had become "my Lady," a saint or special angel who was his teacher and guide lifting him up in the spiritual realm. While camped out in the forests of the Biltmore Estate, he wrote, "Read in St. John in the morning alone and my Lady was there. Went off again in the afternoon and read and my Dear Lady was beautifully there, and we had the most happy time. She spoke to me again and filled me and warmed me. She and God" (April 22, 1896).

To feel Laura's presence and be spiritually married required solitude, study, and quiet contemplation. Because Gifford lived a public life, this was not easy. As a result, some of his most vivid encounters with Laura occurred during the solitude he found while travelling alone on trains.

Gifford's studies consisted of reading books about God, Heaven, and the afterlife to uplift his spiritual consciousness to the level of Laura's. He believed that Laura was reading them with him. Once he read a book "My Lady did not approve of." He was filled with remorse and wrote how very sorry he was. The next day she forgave him, and he wrote of his gratitude for Laura's great goodness.

Gifford was not content just to communicate with Laura. He wanted a complete and permanent reunion and worked to make it happen. He called it "the good time" or "the good thing," and he believed that it was coming very soon. "Laura spoke to me again saying it would not be long" (June 13, 1894); "The good thing is surely coming" (July 5, 1894); "My Lady spoke to me again and I think this is the beginning of the good time" (August 1, 1894); "It will not be long" (January 25, 1895); "The promise is so sure" (March 29, 1895); and "On the train while reading a short life of Emerson, I suddenly had the thought that I must catch up quickly, for the end of my probation is not far off. Surely it came from my Dearest. I am very happy tonight" (March 29, 1895).

These are the most mysterious passages in the diaries and seem to imply that Gifford anticipated leaving the human experience altogether in the very near future. Somehow through spiritual study, he would rise above his human body and life and become one with Laura and God for eternity.

As he wrote on May 4, 1896, "One beautiful moment in the afternoon. I think it meant that I was right in believing that the natural body is not raised, but a wholly spiritual body." Gifford hoped that his spiritual body would be raised to the level of Laura's as soon as possible.

What incredible love Gifford had for Laura to want to leave his family and friends, his successful career, his crusade for forestry, and his growing fame to be with her now and forever, somewhere in the spiritual world beyond the grave. Being with Laura had become more important to him than all his goals and successes. How he expected this "good thing" to happen and "the good time" to come is part of the mystery. Would he die or simply vanish from human view?

The books that Gifford and Laura had read together during Laura's last months at Strawberry Hill and at Uncle Frank's house included the essays of Ralph Waldo Emerson and those of Emanuel Swedenborg and two of the most metaphysical books of the Bible: The Gospel of John and Revelations. Some of the books they read are long forgotten and seldom read: *Science and a Future Life* (1893) by W. H. Myers, *The Choir Invisible* (1897) by James Allen Lane, *The Gates Ajar* (1873) and *Beyond the Gates* (1883) by Elizabeth Stuart Phelps, and *After Her Death* (1897) by Lillian Whiting, to name a few.

A common theme runs through these other now obscure nineteenth-century works: when a loved one dies, that person has not left us. Although in heaven and invisible, our beloved still loves us and helps us and will be waiting to greet us when we too pass into the spiritual realm.

In *After Her Death*, Lillian Whiting instructed her readers on how to communicate with someone whom we love who has died: "The only true, permanent, and satisfactory way to live in companionship and communion with those who have passed through the experience of death is to live in the spirit, to live now and here, every day and every hour, the spiritual life. . . . The problem of communication with those who have passed into the unseen lies with us, rather than with them; it lies in our own purification and exaltation of Life." This passage seems to describe how Gifford reached Laura.

Emanuel Swedenborg was Gifford's favorite author. The writings of Swedenborg that Gifford and Laura most likely read together were *Our Life after Death* and *The Delights of Wisdom Pertaining to Conjugal Love*.[9]

In *The Delights of Wisdom Pertaining to Conjugal Love* (1765), Swedenborg wrote: "Marriages contracted in the world are for the most part external and at the same time internal, when nevertheless it is the internal union, which is of the souls, which really constitutes marriage. . . . No other partners, these are not even called two, but one angel. . . . The spirit of the deceased partner dwells constantly with the one angel. . . . The spirit of the deceased partner dwells constantly with the spirit of the partner still living and does so to the latter's death, when they meet again, are reunited, and love each other more tenderly than they did before, being in the spiritual world. . . . If they do contract something like marriage, they do so for reasons aside from [true] marital love, and these reasons are all external."

During the years that Laura was a divine presence in his life, Gifford believed the inspiration Laura gave him was at least partly, if not entirely, responsible for his most famous successes. For example, after a speech in Philadelphia on January 18, 1896, he wrote, "I spoke as my Lady's servant" and after testifying as Chief Forester of the Forest Service before a Senate Committee on March 24, 1906, "I felt today my Lady's help."

A core belief of Spiritualism is that individuals survive the death of their body by ascending into a spirit existence. A person's condition after death is directly related to the moral quality of his human existence. Communion with the spiritual world is both possible and desirable, and spiritual healing is the natural result of such communication. Spiritualists understand God as infinite intelligence.[10]

Spiritualism had a large following in the late nineteenth and early twentieth centuries.[11] In the mid-1890s, when Gifford and Laura spent time together reading spiritual literature, there were 150 Spiritualist societies in Britain; by 1908, there would be almost 400.[12] Mediums, mostly women, held séances to assist believers in sending or receiving a message to his or her departed loved ones.

As a movement, American Spiritualism dated its inception to 1848 in upstate New York, along with the Women's Rights Movement. All Spiritualists advocated women's rights and equality to men within Spiritualist practice, polity, and ideology.[13] In the 1890s, Susan B. Anthony, Charlotte Perkins Gilman, and Margaret Sanger, leaders of the movement, attended a special Woman Suffrage Day at Lily Dale, a resort for Spiritualists.[14]

Quakers were also drawn to Spiritualism.[15] Women were thought to be especially blessed with possessing "light," the ability to contact the spiritual world.[16]

As writer Ann Braude points out, "Spiritualism's enduring appeal . . . lay in its unique ability to satisfy the one dear hope that no other movement could: the abolition of death."[17]

Spiritualism especially attracted those who had lost beloved ones. Gifford and Laura were not so unusual in their religious beliefs at the time that they read together as it might seem to us today. Several other successful and admired people of their era, most notably Queen Victoria and Mary Todd Lincoln, shared their beliefs about the afterlife.

Ralph Waldo Emerson, another well-known example, was the leader of a group of nineteenth-century Transcendentalists greatly influenced by the work of Emanuel Swedenborg. One of Emerson's essays that Gifford and Laura undoubtedly read was "Uses of Great Men." Emerson chose men to describe those whom he believed to be *"representative."* Swedenborg was the representative of "the mystic."

Laura and Gifford may together have read Oliver Wendell Holmes's biography of Emerson, published in 1885, but we definitely know that Gifford read a short biography of Emerson on March 29, 1895, soon after Laura's death, because he noted it in his diary.

No one made adverse judgments when Emerson married Ellen Tucker when she was in the final stages of consumption. Indeed, "it was a commonplace of popular literature for a bride to die of consumption on or immediately after the wedding day, the bridal dress turned into a shroud or winding-sheet."[18]

Emerson always cherished this first wife, who died seventeen months after their marriage. He and Ellen believed in the eternal life of the soul and that they would meet again in Heaven. Two hours after her last breath, Emerson wrote to his aunt, "My angel is gone to heaven this morning and I am alone in the world and strangely happy."

Emerson biographer Gay Wilson Allen comments about this letter: "In the secular twentieth century, Emerson's strange 'happiness' seems like a morbid perversion, . . . but it should be understood in the context of the religious faith Emerson had been expressing for several months in his sermons and private Journal."[19]

Tuberculosis was endemic in the Emerson family. Two of Waldo's brothers died of consumption, and he was thought to have recovered from a bout of it himself in his youth. The spiritual relationship of Gifford and Laura is remarkably similar to that of the brilliant Charles Emerson, the youngest and favorite brother of Waldo, who was in love with the beautiful Elizabeth, daughter of Concord's most important citizen, Samuel Hoar. The couple was engaged to be married and had planned to live together with Waldo and his second wife, Lidian, in their home that was being enlarged to fit the joint family.[20]

Unfortunately, Charles died several months before the wedding was scheduled to take place. Elizabeth, however, considered herself Charles's wife and never married, despite her parents' disapproval of her stubbornness and the solicitations of a number of suitors. In their letters to each other, Charles and Elizabeth, just like Gifford and Laura, shared a strong belief in an afterlife in which they would meet again. For the rest of her life, Elizabeth remained attached to the Emerson family, serving as Waldo's amanuensis and poetic muse and helping Lidian, like a dear maiden aunt, with the couple's children.[21]

Gifford and Laura were probably also aware of the writings of Sir Arthur Conan Doyle, whose novels were published in the 1880s. Although Doyle claimed in his autobiography that he remained an agnostic from the time he received his medical degree in 1881 until his conversion to Spiritualism in 1916, he studied and was attracted to the teachings and practices of Spiritualism from as early as 1880. In fact, it was in 1887, shortly after writing *A Study in Scarlet*, that Doyle wrote two letters to the weekly Spiritualist periodical *Light* in which he recounted his conversion to Spiritualism.

As a result of his experiences, Doyle was convinced that "it is absolutely certain that intelligence can exist apart from the body." "After weighing the evidence," he wrote, "I could no more doubt the existence of the phenomena than I could doubt the existence of lions in Africa, though I have been to that continent and have never chanced to see one." He also exhorted "any other searcher never to despair of receiving personal testimony but to persevere through any number of failures until at last conviction comes to him, as, it will."[22]

In 1882, Doyle was one of the founders of the Society for
Psychical Research, along with Sir William Barrett, professor
of physics at the Royal College of Science in Dublin; philoso-
pher Henry Sidgwick; Edmund Gurney; and Sir Oliver Lodge,
a British physicist and writer involved in the development of
key patents in wireless telegraphy. These and other scientists
and philosophers wished to bring scientific scrutiny to ghosts,
séances, telepathy, and other paranormal events. Theirs was
the first society to conduct organized scholarly research into
human experiences that challenged contemporary scientific
models. The society's mission was to investigate allegations
of such phenomena in order to expose the fraudulent and to
verify authentic supernatural occurrences. Many of the founders were Spiritualists, hoping to "combat the mockery of their
faith."[23] Its membership included some of the most important
British men of the era, among them John Ruskin, H. G. Wells,
and Prime Ministers Arthur Balfour and William E. Glad-
stone.[24] Among those corresponding members who contributed articles and letters to its *Proceedings* were Sigmund Freud
and Carl Jung.[25]

William James, one of the most influential thinkers of the
early twentieth century and author of *The Varieties of Religious
Experience* and the spiritualist book *Human Immortality*, was
one of the founders of an American branch of the society, also
in 1882. Samuel Clemens (better known as Mark Twain) was
an early member.

In the summer of 1894, James was named the society's
president. As Professor of Psychology at Harvard, he believed
research into such topics as telepathy, clairvoyance, and me-
diumship was an extension of abnormal psychology.[26] Investi-

gating such topics interested him for the rest of his life.[27] James wanted "to investigate so-called spirit phenomena by the same strictly empirical methods one would use for any other phenomena."[28]

James had discovered a trance medium, Leonora Piper, and observed her trances "a dozen times" and sent twenty other people to observe her.[29] His conclusion was "I cannot resist the conviction that knowledge appears which she has never gained by the ordinary waking use of her eyes and ears and wits." Members of the Psychology Department of Clark University, G. S. Hall and Amy Tanner, conducted experiments on Mrs. Piper. For twenty-five years, the Society for Psychical Research paid Mrs. Piper a salary and oversaw her activities so that its researchers could study the trances of the medium in a controlled, scientific environment.[30]

One of the financial supporters of the American branch of the society was heiress Theodate Pope (later, Riddle). She was the only child of Quaker businessman Alfred A. Pope, president of the National Malleable and Steel Casting Company and collector of French Impressionist art, with his wife, Ada. Theodate grew up on Euclid Avenue, "Millionaires' Row" in Cleveland, where the Hannas, Sherwins, and Rockefellers all had large mansions.[31]

In Farmington, Connecticut, where she had gone to school, Theodate built a house called Hill-Stead; it is still there and is a museum open to the public. There, she entertained many important friends, including some active in American Spiritualism, such as the artist Mary Cassatt and professor and author William James as well as his brother Henry. When in Cambridge, Theodore routinely stayed with the James family.

Theodore Roosevelt's sister Anna was a neighbor and friend. Theodate Pope Riddle became one of the first female licensed architects and designed the restoration of the birthplace of Roosevelt in Manhattan.

Theodore met with Harvard professor Dr. Richard Hodgson, who had joined the American Society for Psychical Research in 1887 to serve as its secretary. He arranged for sittings between her and Mrs. Piper.

In 1914, Theodore met Edwin Friend, a Spiritualist who had taught at the University of Berlin and at Princeton, who was conducting psychical research at Harvard. The two decided to meet with members of the English Society for Psychical Research, despite the risk of traveling during World War I. They boarded the *Lusitania*, and Friend perished when a German U-boat torpedoed and sank the ship on May 7, 1915. Theodore was rescued and returned to America.

GIFFORD'S CAREER
AFTER LAURA'S DEATH

Gifford did not outwardly appear to grieve Laura's death. Immediately after the memorial service, he returned to New York and went back to work at his forester's office, answering the backlog of mail. He apologized for his tardiness by explaining that there had been "an illness in the family." Mary Pinchot's faith that her son would overcome the tragedy appeared justified much more quickly than she and the rest of his family and friends could have hoped.

Four days after Laura's death, Marcia Houghteling sent Gifford a note from Uncle Frank's house, "We shall always have so much in common that we must try to see each other often. Make our house your house whenever you can and believe me [to be] your ever loving friend."

Gifford took Mrs. Houghteling at her word and actually moved the belongings that he used in Asheville to Strawberry Hill, calling it "home."[1] Laura's relatives soon became his relatives and Mrs. Houghteling became "Mother," a name he had not called her before Laura's death and never used in connection with his own mother, whom he called "Mamee."

In his diary, Gifford always indicated the place where he was staying. Many of the diary entries for 1894 and 1895 are listed as from Strawberry Hill.[2] Thus, we can assume that Gifford stayed with Mrs. Houghteling during the spring of 1894 when he made several trips to look over a tract of eighty-odd thousand acres George Vanderbilt was thinking of buying. The land was adjacent to the Pink Beds, a lush area of cove forests and streams near Brevard, ranging in elevation from 2,000 feet to 6,410 feet. The area is named for the profusion of pink wildflowers, including mountain laurel and rhododendron, that appear in the spring.

"It was a superb region of sharp ridges, steep slopes and narrow valleys. In its coves Chestnut [then the most numerous species!] Red Oak, White Oak, and Yellow Poplar were the principal lumber trees. The high percentage of mature timber offered a fine chance for profitable Forestry," Pinchot wrote to his employer. "I recommended the purchase. To say that I am delighted with the whole area is to put it mildly." Early in 1895 George Vanderbilt took it over and named it Pisgah Forest.[3]

Vanderbilt took the name from the most prominent mountain in the area closest to Biltmore: Mount Pisgah. He purchased the 300 acres comprising the mountain from Senator Thomas L. Clingman for $800.[4] During 1893 and 1894, Mary Lusk, granddaughter of speculator Zechariah Candler, sold more than 50,000 acres of inherited land near Mount Pisgah to Vanderbilt for $35,000.[5]

In 1895, Pinchot and the German forester Dr. Carl Alwin Schenck scouted Pisgah Ridge and surrounding woodlands, the Pink Beds, and Big Creek Valley to discuss plans for expansion of Vanderbilt's forests. Schenck had been hired in that year to replace Pinchot, because the work on Vanderbilt's expanding property required a full-time resident forester and Pinchot's business as a consulting forester in New York was expanding to claim more of his time.

On horseback, the two men climbed the steep route from Hominy Valley to Buck Spring Gap that had been carved yearly by livestock herded to high-ridge meadows.[6] Vanderbilt named the path they followed from the Biltmore Estate to Mount Pisgah the "Shut-in Trail" for the ridge that it ascends. The ridge had been named nearly a century earlier for the fact that it "shut in" the Bent Creek valley from the adjacent French Broad River valley. The name also referred to the fact that parts of the trail wend through what are called "rhododendron hells." The rhododendron grow closely together and form a canopy overhead, making the hiker feel shut in. The Shut-in Trail would be used by thousands of hikers in the following century and beyond.

The two men camped at the foot of Mount Pisgah in a hut built for Pinchot's bear-hunting trips, which he called "Good Enough Cabin."[7] In 1910, on the same site, architect Richard Morris Hunt designed a group of Adirondack-style log cabins that Vanderbilt named Buck Spring Lodge. It comprised ten buildings including a main lodge, a kitchen/dining room, a stable, a garage, a honeymoon cottage, and a playhouse/school for Vanderbilt's daughter. Outbuildings included a cellar and a springhouse. Those buildings were demolished in the 1960s.

The Biltmore Estate became well known as a center of forestry and forest preservation, in part as a result of Pinchot's work there. Young men with collegiate education sought training and experience in its woodlands and in the forest school established by Schenck. Biltmore had become a Mecca for advocates of scientific forestry and the conservation movement.[8]

Even before he opened his New York office in December 1893, Pinchot had been asked by W. Seward Webb, Vanderbilt's brother-in-law, to examine a large area in the Adirondacks that he owned in order to ascertain the advisability of applying forest management methods there. This led to an opportunity for Pinchot to introduce scientific forestry into several other areas of Adirondack woodlands owned by wealthy men as well as the state-owned forest preserve that had been established there in 1885.[9]

A forestry meeting held in Albany from March 6–8, 1894, just a month after Laura's death, was Pinchot's first major opportunity to be heard by prominent advocates of forest preservation in New York, Pennsylvania, and from the federal government and to influence public policy concerning forests.

In 1896, Pinchot was appointed secretary of the National Forest Commission and served on a committee to make a preliminary report and recommendation, with the support of President Grover Cleveland. During three months in the summer of 1896, Pinchot and several other members of the Commission visited federal forest areas in the West, accompanied by John Muir. Pinchot and his fellow Yale alumnus Henry S. Graves, now a trained forester, traveled by horseback rather than by train to study the effects of fire, lumbering, and grazing.

The commission's report, presented to newly installed President William McKinley on May 1, 1897, recommended the establishment of a forestry bureau in the US Department of the Interior. The report brought Pinchot to national attention as the foremost authority on the condition of American forests.

Cornelius Bliss, the Secretary of the Interior, appointed Pinchot as a special forest agent to examine and report on eighteen western forests in the summer of 1897.[10]

Pinchot became Chief of the Division of Forestry of the US Department of Agriculture on July 1, 1898, when Bernhard Fernow, who did not believe in the feasibility of forest management by the federal government, resigned. Because the forest reserves were still under the jurisdiction of the Department of the Interior, the Agriculture Department's Forestry Division controlled not a single acre of forests. However, Pinchot directed the division, and later in 1900 the new Bureau of Forestry,[11] to educate the general public and the forest industry on the practicality of scientific forestry by offering the services of federal foresters to timber companies. Pinchot began investigations in fire protection and reforestation.

In October 1898, the Division of Forestry offered to help owners of private forestlands by making working plans for management of their property for conservation. This service was free to small landowners, and those with large tracts simply had to pay for expenses. Within ten years, the agency received 938 formal applications for forest management assistance on some eight million acres all across the nation.[12]

Pinchot then initiated a program of research to deal with the need for more scientific knowledge of the production characteristics and potentials of American forests—studies and methods of application that continue in place to this day. The division produced many reports on various eastern trees such as yellow poplar, black walnut, pencil cedar, and bald cypress, and western ones such as Douglas fir, coastal redwood, giant cedar, and several pines.

Along with silviculture research, Pinchot also concentrated on methods to promote forest protection. Control of insect damage was a subject of ongoing research. Studies were also performed on fire, including the extent and damage done by forest fires, detailed studies of the effect of fires upon future forests, and the best methods for prevention and control of forest fires.[13]

Pinchot's staff grew. The young foresters from the division who worked with the private landowners became, in effect, missionaries for scientific forestry and conservation. They were sometimes referred to as "Pinchot's Young Men." They frequently were invited to the "Chief's" home after regular working hours for a meal of gingerbread, baked apples, and milk. He gave them inspiring talks to spur them on in their work.[14]

Forestry as a profession came of age during the Progressive Era. At Pinchot's urging, New York State established the Cornell Forest School in 1898. In 1900, he and his parents contributed an endowment of $150,000—later increased to $300,000—as the basis for a school of forestry at Yale, and the American Forestry Association raised $125,000 to endow a chair at the new school. In 1903, Pinchot was elected Professor of Forestry in the Forest School; he was responsible for giving a short course of lectures each year.[15]

A summer session for first-year Yale students was set up at Grey Towers. One of the early students, a graduate of the class of 1909, was Aldo Leopold. He later joined the US Forest Service and served in Arizona and New Mexico. By the age of twenty-four, Leopold had been promoted to the post of supervisor for the Carson National Forest in New Mexico. In 1922, he was instrumental in developing the proposal to manage the

Gila National Forest as a wilderness area, which became the first such official designation in 1924. Leopold is remembered today as the author of *A Sand County Almanac* and as one of the country's first true environmental ethicists. In 1935, he became director of the Audubon Society and founded the Wilderness Society.

Through force of his personality and belief in scientific forestry, Gifford Pinchot attracted several other knowledgeable young men to the Bureau, many of them graduates of Yale and Cornell.

Just ten days before the end of his term in office in 1897, President Grover Cleveland created thirteen new forest reserves in South Dakota, Wyoming, Montana, Idaho, Washington, California, and Utah, without consulting the states involved or their congressmen. Cleveland, thus, inadvertently created permanent enemies of federal forest policy and the conservation movement in these western states.[16]

Many people there resented government regulations of forests and restrictions on mining and agriculture, especially on grazing land for cattle and sheep. Many of the westerners believed that the forests should not be kept as untouched reserves and saved from commercial use as parks or areas of natural beauty or to protect watersheds. As historian Thomas Wellock points out, "The early practices, leadership, and public support for conservation policies emerged in the Northeast. . . . A conservation philosophy formulated in the East was bound to run into trouble when implemented west of the Mississippi."[17]

President Cleveland's last-minute creation of forest reserves created a long-lasting problem for Pinchot, and he spent the next decade dealing with it. During the years between 1898 and 1905, he worked to influence Congress to move the responsibility for the national forests from the Department of Interior to the Department of Agriculture so that the reserves could be opened more fully to commercial use, including limited grazing.

In March 1903, Pinchot addressed the Society of American Foresters, saying, "The object of our forest policy is not to preserve forests because they are beautiful . . . or because they are refuges for the wild creatures of the wilderness . . . but for the making of prosperous homes. . . . Every other consideration comes as secondary."[18]

Pinchot readily admitted that the immediate economic results of the introduction of scientific forestry methods were low, and in most cases detailed cost and benefit figures were not available. However, one example was the 6,500-acre forest of the University of the South at Sewanee, Tennessee, which reported that in seven years lumber from this tract had yielded a net profit of almost $13,000, whereas normal logging in the area would have brought a fair value of only $2,000.[19]

By 1900, lumbermen became much more interested in using existing forests more sustainably, as virgin forests were no longer available, having all been previously cut over. They became active in the American Forestry Association, a group that supported the future US Forest Service in the Department of Agriculture.[20]

THE ADMINISTRATION
OF PRESIDENT
THEODORE ROOSEVELT

I n his book *City of Ambition: FDR, LaGuardia, and the Making of Modern New York* (New York, W. W. Norton & Company, 2013), Mason B. Williams looks back and defines the central beliefs of the Progressive Era (1890–1920): "Society could be improved through concerted human action; that advances in technology, engineering, and medicine had opened the door to unprecedented social progress; and that it was the task of government to help American society adapt to the new technological age." Both Gifford Pinchot and Theodore Roosevelt fervently shared these beliefs.

On February 5, 1899, the newly elected Governor of New York invited Pinchot to stay overnight in the Governor's Mansion in Albany. The two men shared a similar background as sons of wealthy and influential Eastern families, and both had

a love of the outdoors and vigorous activities. This was the beginning of a long friendship and alliance for conservation.

Before dinner the two men boxed and wrestled.[1] As Harold K.
Steen, the editor of Pinchot's *Conservation Diaries*, wrote of
their friendship, "This sort of manly gusto would become the
trademark of their ever-closer relationship, as their frequent
tennis matches, vigorous hikes and horseback rides, and just
plain chopping wood and picnicking at Sagamore Hill, the
president's Long Island home, provided opportunities to discuss world matters on a presidential scale, and for the forester
to offer advice that the president sought. In a town that mea-
sures influence in units of access, as does Washington, DC,
Pinchot and the Forest Service acquired a temporary level of
influence that has not been achieved by any other agency, or
its chief, since."[2]

During his tenure as governor of New York, Roosevelt had
persuaded the legislature to preserve tens of thousands of for-
ested acres in the Catskills and the Adirondacks. His second
annual message about conservation was so important that,
"Pinchot committed whole passages to memory 'as if it were
the Gettysburg Address,'" while ornithologists considered its
call for the protection of endangered birds 'the tipping point
for the Audubon Movement.'"[3]

Upon the assassination of William McKinley on September 14, 1901, Theodore Roosevelt became the twenty-sixth and
youngest US president and then was elected for two additional
terms, serving until March 4, 1909.

Although Roosevelt fully supported Pinchot's policies and
methods for the protection and conservation of forests, and
there was increasing national support, Pinchot had to deal

with constant criticism from western interests. They wanted to use federal forest resources without government regulations, especially for mining and agriculture.

Pinchot was adept at using public relations and any other means to fight his critics. He developed an extensive publicity program that included press releases to newspapers, provision of technical information to individuals, loan of slides and pictures to lecturers and writers, public lectures, and provision of materials for use in schools, from elementary to college level.

The first federal forest experiment station was created in 1908 near Flagstaff, Arizona, and a second station was built in Colorado. A program of regional forest and range experimental stations was set up to conduct broad research for solution of problems specific to that area.[4] Pinchot made frequent on-the-ground inspections of these stations to get out in the field and to keep in touch with their activities.

Pinchot was involved in the convening, from January 2–6, 1905, of the American Forest Congress in Washington, DC, to discuss the need for forest preservation and to promote the transfer of care of the forest reserves from the Department of the Interior to the Department of Agriculture's new US Forest Service, which President Roosevelt accomplished that year. Pinchot had been working toward this goal for seven years, trying to persuade congressmen and enlisting the aid of influential railroad, mining, and lumber companies.[5] Pinchot led this new agency as its first chief, charged with caring for the newly renamed national forests. Pinchot would eventually be responsible for the administration of nearly 200,000 acres of forestland.[6]

This appointment led to an increasing battle between Congress versus Pinchot and Roosevelt over management of the nation's forests. Congressmen, and particularly those from the western states, were opposed to what they called "Pinchotism." They resented the fact that Pinchot and Roosevelt were eastern, wealthy, and aristocratic and proposed "grandiose plans." Roosevelt, they thought, believed the US president could do anything he wanted unless the Constitution prohibited it, whereas they believed that the executive government could only do what the Constitution already defined or Congress had established by law.

On February 25, 1907, influenced by western lumbering interests opposed to Pinchot's conservation philosophy, the Senate passed an amendment to the Agriculture Appropriations Act, rescinding the president's executive power to designate national forests in western states and transferring the power to Congress, as Roosevelt claimed, "to be exploited by land grabbers and by the representatives of the great special interests." He and Pinchot "devised an ingenious remedy."

Pinchot and his staff worked forty-eight hours straight to draft proclamations placing all sixteen million acres of six western states into forestlands. Roosevelt immediately signed an executive order withdrawing the lands from development and in effect designating nearly three-dozen new national forests.[7]

Roosevelt also appointed Pinchot to the Inland Waterways Commission, created by Congress in March 1907, at the request of the president, to investigate the transportation crisis that recently had affected the nation's ability to move its produce and industrial production efficiently. The immediate crisis centered on insufficient railroad capacity developed by the private sector and competing but neglected inland shipping.

Roosevelt's progressive conservationist interest was focused more than on transportation alone. The president wanted water projects to be considered for their multiple uses and in relation to other natural resources. He asked for a comprehensive plan for the improvement and control of the river systems of the United States. Pinchot was one of the most active members of the Inland Waterways Commission.

That same year, Roosevelt issued invitations to the governors of the states and territories to a Conference of Governors, to be held in the White House, May 13–15, 1908. Pinchot was the primary mover of the conference and largely financed it himself. He hoped to convince the governors to agree with his belief in the scientific and efficient management of natural resources on the federal level. This 1908 meeting was the beginning of the annual governors' conferences, now held by the National Governors Association.

The focus of the conference was on natural resources and their proper use. Roosevelt delivered the opening address: "Conservation as a National Duty." Among those speaking were leading industrialists, such as Andrew Carnegie and James J. Hill, politicians, and natural resource experts. Their speeches emphasized both the nation's need to exploit renewable resources and the differing situations of the various states, requiring different plans.

This conference was a seminal event in the history of conservationism; it brought the issue to public attention in a highly visible way. The next year saw two outgrowths of the Conference: the National Conservation Commission, which Roosevelt and Pinchot set up with representatives from the states and federal agencies, and the First National Conservation Congress, which Pinchot led, as an assembly of private conservation interests.

The National Conservation Commission was appointed in June by the president, chaired by Pinchot, and composed of representatives of Congress and relevant executive agencies. It compiled an inventory of US natural resources and presented Pinchot's concept of resource management as a comprehensive policy recommendation in a three-volume report submitted to Congress at the beginning of 1909.

"Conservation stands for development," Pinchot wrote in the report. "Conservation demands the welfare of this generation first, and afterward the welfare of the generations to follow. . . . The natural resources must be developed and preserved for the benefit of the many, and not merely for the profit of a few."

Pinchot agreed to draft a chapter on conservation during Roosevelt's presidency for Roosevelt's autobiography. Roosevelt was generous in his assessment of Pinchot's work, "among the many, many public officials who under my administration rendered literally invaluable service to the people of the United States, he, on the whole, stood first." As Steen writes, "What bureau chief could hope for more?"[8]

Indeed, during Roosevelt's presidency (1901–1909), he and Pinchot were able to bring together many competing conservation efforts to establish scientific forestry, dam projects, irrigation proposals, and wildlife management for the general good.

A catalog of their accomplishments is indeed impressive. With Pinchot at his side, Roosevelt established five national parks, sixteen national monuments, and fifty-three wildlife reserves. Roosevelt ran with the wide latitude afforded him under the Antiquities Act of 1906 to designate as national monuments "objects of historic or scientific interest." While Congress intended the law to protect only small areas around artifacts, such as Indian cliff dwellings in the Southwest, Roosevelt used it for scenic preservation, establishing hundreds of thousands of acres of the Grand Canyon and Washington's Olympic peninsula as "monuments." Monuments often became national parks, once political sentiment caught up with Roosevelt's actions. But the chief winner of the president's actions was the forest reserve system. When Roosevelt moved into the White House in 1901, there were 41 national forest reserves encompassing 41 million acres. By 1909, there were 159 national forests containing 150 million acres.[9]

THE ADMINISTRATION OF PRESIDENT WILLIAM H. TAFT

William Taft and Theodore Roosevelt had become friends during Taft's tenure as solicitor general under President William Henry Harrison. After filling legal posts in his hometown of Cincinnati, Taft had been appointed by President William McKinley as governor general of the Philippines, where he served with distinction. Back in Washington, DC, by 1904, Taft became T. R.'s secretary of war. Two years later, as Roosevelt's term was ending, he offered Taft the choice to serve as either president or chief justice; Taft chose the court, which had been his dream for years. However, following a private meeting between Taft's wife, Nellie, and Roosevelt, Taft was swayed into running for the US presidency instead. Taft had an easy victory in the November 1908 election, sliding in on Roosevelt's popularity and endorsement. He was sworn in as president on March 4, 1909.

Even before the election, Gifford Pinchot and other conservationists worried about whether the new president would support their views and programs as much as Roosevelt had. In haste, they made plans and issued directives, hoping that they could make their policies invulnerable from the attacks of an administration that might want to rescind them.

Their worries were justified by a December 1908 speech by Taft in which he said, "There is one difficulty about the conservation of natural resources. It is that the imagination of those who are pressing it may outrun the practical facts."[1]

In the summer of 1909, Pinchot had organized the National Conservation Commission to create widespread popular support for the Roosevelt conservation policies.[2]

Many years later, Pinchot contrasted Taft's presidency with that of Roosevelt: "Taft's so-called judicial temperament, much lauded during his campaign, leading as it did to an insistence on limiting his defense of the public interest in terms of precedent and strictly-construed legal mandates, was one of the most important lines of demarcation between himself and Roosevelt. The latter . . . held that under all circumstances the public good comes first. He saw himself as the active and aggressive champion of the public welfare who looked upon impartiality between right and wrong, between the people and the plunderers, as little better than treachery. Taft on the other hand, regarded himself as an impartial judge acting under the letter of the law."[3]

In other words, Taft believed in a strict interpretation of the Constitution, that the president can only do what the Constitution defines or what is specifically authorized by law, whereas Roosevelt's view was that the federal government could proceed with projects it deemed as supporting the public good unless the Constitution prohibited such action.

Pinchot cited Jefferson's Louisiana Purchase, Lincoln's Emancipation Proclamation, and Roosevelt's own construction of the Panama Canal as examples. Roosevelt had always been the man of action.

The two presidents differed over important natural resource laws, too: Taft disagreed with new hydroelectric, oil, and coal land policies. Taft immediately dismissed several Roosevelt appointees, including conservationist Assistant Attorney General for the Department of Interior George Woodruff "who received a 'promotion' to the post of federal judge in Hawaii."[4]

However, no appointment would have more far-reaching consequences for Pinchot in Taft's administration than his decision to replace Interior Secretary James Garfield with Richard A. Ballinger, a corporation lawyer and mayor of Seattle. Earlier, Roosevelt had urged his friend to keep Garfield, and Taft had previously said that he would.[5]

Under Roosevelt, the relationship between Pinchot in Agriculture and Garfield in Interior had been cordial and informal; they agreed on many issues.[6] One of Ballinger's first acts was to insist that communications between Pinchot and some of the agencies in the Department of the Interior should first go through the Secretary of Agriculture to Ballinger and then to the agencies under him. However, animosity between Pinchot and the new Interior Secretary Ballinger soon flared into open discord.

Pinchot concluded that Taft and Ballinger were "at least partly complicit in what he believed was a fraudulent transfer of federal coal land in Alaska to the Morgan-Guggenheim syndicate. Pinchot believed that such a transfer was a violation of 'the people's interest.'"

Taft and Ballinger refused to investigate the claims of fraud.[7] "Taft dismissed the meddlesome Pinchot as 'too much of a radical and a crank' who saw conspiracies everywhere."[8]

The many details of the Ballinger-Pinchot Affair are beyond the scope of our story. Many books have been written treating in detail all that happened and why it was significant. It was, in essence, a conflict rooted in contrasting ideals about how to best use and conserve western natural resources. The conflict quickly escalated beyond the confines of a mere personal squabble into a matter of national importance. The Ballinger-Pinchot scandal erupted when an article in *Colliers* magazine accused Secretary Ballinger of shady dealings in Alaskan coal lands. Newspapers across the country featured daily stories as the scandal unfolded.[9]

Taft decided to remove Pinchot from his post for insubordination, writing in a letter to him on January 10, 1910, "by your own conduct you have destroyed your usefulness as a helpful subordinate of the Government."[10]

Rather than resigning, Pinchot had actually tried to force Taft to fire him and was delighted when he did. Once out of the Taft administration, he was able to bring his views to the public. He traveled widely across the country, outlining his views about the controversy and explaining the conservation policy that he had followed under Roosevelt and with his support. As Pinchot wrote, "Taft was on trial before the jury of the people as to whether or not the much-admired T. R. policies were safe in his hands."[11]

After the new president was sworn in, Roosevelt and his son Kermit had departed for a long vacation on safari in Africa and later touring Europe. While there, he had received "numerous disturbing communications from his progressive friends."[12]

Word that Taft had fired Gifford Pinchot left Roosevelt dumbfounded. "I do not know any man in public life who has rendered quite the service you have rendered," he wrote to Pinchot, "and it seems to me absolutely impossible that there can be any truth in this statement." When the news was confirmed, he asked Pinchot to meet him in Europe in order to hear his firsthand account.[13]

While in Africa, Roosevelt had learned little of Taft's administrative troubles. Pinchot spent a whole day with T. R. at his villa on the Italian Riviera in mid-April and gave him all the details while the two went on a long trek over the Maritime Alps.

Months earlier, Pinchot had enumerated Taft's failings in a letter, condemning the new president's decision to surround himself with corporate lawyers, his surrender of executive powers to Congress, and, most damningly, his appointment of Richard Ballinger.

"We have fallen back down the hill you led us up," Pinchot had written in the letter, "and there is a general belief that the special interests are once more substantially in full control of both Congress and the administration."[14]

With Roosevelt's allies falling in behind Pinchot, and Taft defending Ballinger, the controversy would pit the East of America versus the West, corporate interests against public rights, developers against conservationists—until all the divisive factions at play in the confrontation between Pinchot and Ballinger were framed as the opening volley in the battle for the 1912 presidential nomination.[15]

Pinchot had helped craft a modern state capable of managing and regulating natural resources. He gave the American people an understanding of the importance of conservation and was the first to use this term publicly. He had a large national following who viewed him as a hero.

By the early twentieth century, a large section of the population supported Pinchot's view that the federal government was to keep, administer, and manage the public lands for the benefit of the greatest number, a huge extension in federal power and a remarkable shift in public opinion.[16]

Interestingly, members of the Sierra Club supported Roosevelt over Taft in this fracas, despite the then-current clash over the proposed inundation of the Hetch Hetchy Valley, which Roosevelt and Pinchot supported. As Char Williams writes, "The organization rallied to Pinchot's side in the aftermath of the Ballinger affair. On May Day, 1910, three hundred members of the club hiked into Muir Woods and christened a most perfect specimen of a coastal redwood the Pinchot Memorial Tree." A bronze plaque on a nearby rock proclaimed the inscription: "This tree is dedicated to GIFFORD PINCHOT Friend of the Forest, Conserver of the common-wealth."[17]

MARRIAGE TO CORNELIA BRYCE

M uch of Gifford Pinchot's time and energy after his dismissal from the Forest Service was spent on political activities. The controversy over the Ballinger-Pinchot Affair soon became a major factor in splitting the Republican Party. Theodore Roosevelt concluded that William Taft had so badly betrayed the ethics of conservation that he had to be ousted. Roosevelt mounted a challenge to Taft, the Republican candidate for a second term, on the independent Progressive "Bull Moose" ticket in 1912. Pinchot was, of course, active in support of Roosevelt and gave a total of fifty-four speeches on Roosevelt's behalf. However, the split in the Republican Party between Taft and Roosevelt supporters led to three major candidates vying for the vote and the ultimate election of Democratic candidate Woodrow Wilson.

Gifford first met Cornelia Bryce in 1912 while they were both campaigning for Roosevelt.[1] Cornelia, or "Leila," was raised in a wealthy Victorian tradition, much as Gifford had been, with

FIGURE 8. Cornelia Bryce Pinchot marching in Suffragette Parade in New York City; courtesy of the US Forest Service, Grey Towers National Historic Site.

frequent travel to Europe and between New York City and Newport. She was educated in private schools and enjoyed competitive sports—especially hunting, polo, and driving. Her father, Lloyd Bryce, was an editor for the *North American Review*, paymaster general of New York, and minister to the Netherlands at The Hague. Her mother, Edith Cooper, was the daughter of a New York City mayor and granddaughter of

Peter Cooper—inventor, philanthropist, and founder of Cooper Union, a college of science and engineering, which, until recently, was tuition free.[2]

However, Cornelia did not lead the routine life of a woman of society. Not only was she rich, thirty-three years old, and still unmarried, but also she was one of the nation's most active feminists, often campaigning for suffrage and better working conditions for women, sometimes even picketing at factory gates.

"Her earliest memory of her political heritage was handing out literature in her father's political campaign at the age of six. Cornelia was one of the few persons whose whirlwind energy matched Pinchot's and in Roosevelt's words, 'she had one of the keenest political minds that I have ever known.'"[3]

The first entry in Gifford's diary that mentions Cornelia is on March 15, 1913: "Evening dinner and reception. Peters & others. Miss Bryce came & Mrs. Brooks." Four days later, he writes, "Called on Miss Bryce & Mrs. Brooks." On April 4, he writes, "Dinner at the Norman Whitehouse's. Florence, Miss Bryce, Mrs. Older, etc." On April 8, 1913, at a big dinner in Washington, "Sat between Mrs. Peters & Miss Bryce."

More than two months later, Gifford indicated in his diary that Miss Bryce spent the weekend of June 22–23, 1913, at Grey Towers. They had a picnic and spent the day fishing. They took the train together back to New York on the 24th.

On June 30, Gifford had a talk with his mother: "Evening Mamee & I went over the main dates in the history for the family from 1865 to 1881. That was a good thing to do. I wrote them down."

One can imagine Mrs. Pinchot and Mrs. Bryce negotiating in their townhouse parlors, reminiscent of an Edith Wharton novel. Both had a problem to solve. Gifford, the oldest son, was showing no interest in ever getting married and carrying on the family name, and Cornelia was becoming unmarriageable because of her age and radical views. A marriage between them may have seemed like the perfect solution. This would be a grand alliance of two old and wealthy New York society families.

There was no further mention of Miss Bryce in the diary for some time, although Gifford attended a women's suffrage lunch on January 6, 1914, in Pittsburgh, and was elected vice-president of the Men's Association for Woman Suffrage.

On July 30, 1914, Gifford met "Leila & Miss Ruth Morgan in Philadelphia" and "then drive with Leila in the Park." It was notable that he now wrote of her using her nickname rather than referring to her as "Miss Bryce."

The next day, in Roslyn, New York, "Met Leila" for lunch "& long talk with her." They went by automobile to speak with Mrs. Bryce. "Then a wonderful talk with Leila." On August 1, they took the ferry to Saugatuck, Connecticut, where "I spoke to Mr. Bryce after lunch. Picnic just Leila & I, at Seaman's Rock." They spent the next three days in Saugatuck, and on August 5, Leila left at 8:15. The next day was "The Day of the Final yes."

On August 7, "The good morning letter from Leila. Also another."[4]

On August 15, 1914, Gifford Pinchot married Cornelia Bryce. Gifford was forty-nine years old and Cornelia was thirty-three. Gifford and Cornelia's wedding was simple and rushed, not at all what one might expect for two people of their social status. It had been only nine days before the wedding that Cornelia had given her "final yes." The ceremony at her parents' home on Long Island included only family and a few close friends, along with Theodore Roosevelt.

The wedding took place during the midst of Gifford's first senatorial race. It had been suggested that the campaign was one of the reasons for the decision to wed—and to make use of Cornelia's political skills. "A landslide defeat was not a welcome wedding gift—but did not deflate the Pinchots."[5]

After so many years of total loyalty to Laura, why did Gifford marry? The best explanation is his sense of duty to his family. Gifford was the eldest and the favorite of his parents. They wanted him married with a family. His father had died in 1908 without seeing this accomplished and now his mother was dying. A formidable matriarch, Mary Pinchot made it clear that she wanted to see her beloved Gifford married before she died. There was not much time. Immediately after the wedding, Gifford and Cornelia hurried to her bedside in New York. Nine days later, Mary Pinchot was dead, all her dreams of a successful life for her son fulfilled.

"With wealth, energy, enthusiasm, political ambition, and the stamp of approval from Roosevelt, Cornelia and Gifford were equally matched, and apparently very much in love. (One of Gifford's biographers said he was as much in love as a man half his age.)"[6]

Gifford and Cornelia were married for thirty-two years and had one child, Gifford Bryce Pinchot. By all accounts, the marriage was a success. Cornelia continued to pursue her many causes while at the same time helping Gifford further his career. She supported him in navigating the politics of Pennsylvania during his campaign for the governorship. They were good companions.[7]

FIGURE 9. Cornelia Bryce Pinchot and her husband hunted, fished, and camped together; courtesy of the US Forest Service, Grey Towers National Historic Site.

Gifford had remained faithful to Laura for twenty years. In his article for *Pennsylvania History,* James G. Bradley assumed that Gifford's celibacy probably lasted until he married Cornelia at the age of forty-nine. Because of his love for Laura and his lifetime commitment to moral rectitude and self-discipline, he probably was a virgin on his wedding day. It would seem that in Gifford's mind, he already was married to Laura when he married Cornelia. What few diary entries there are about Cornelia are warm, but without the emotional intensity of those about Laura.

Where was Laura during this courtship, wedding, and long
marriage? Had Gifford stopped loving her? There are compel-
ling reasons to believe that Gifford loved Laura for the rest of
his life. He never threw away their letters, his mementos of her,
or her pictures. He stored them lovingly at Grey Towers in a
blue box ordered from Tiffany's on March 2, 1894, and picked
up on the 8th[8] just for this purpose. The box was still there, bat-
tered and faded when Bradley found it. Inside the blue box was
an old wallet, torn and falling apart. Inside was a folded piece
of paper with an excerpt of the following poem by John Luckey
McCreery, copied in Gifford's handwriting. Gifford must have
treasured the poem, carrying it with him, perhaps every day.

> When beautiful, familiar forms
> That we have learned to love are torn
> From our embracing arms.
>
> They are not dead. They have but passed
> Beyond the mists that blind us here
> Into the new and larger life
> Of that serener sphere.
>
> They have dropped their robe of clay
> To put their shining raiment on
> They have not wandered far away
> They are not lost or gone.
>
> Though disenthralled and glorified
> They still are here and love us yet
> The dear ones they left behind
> They never can forget.

Gifford's diary entries about Laura continued during his courtship with Cornelia almost to the wedding day itself. The last entry is on July 30, 1914, fourteen days before the wedding: "Not a clear day." The fact that they then abruptly stop does not necessarily mean that he was no longer thinking about Laura, but more probably indicate his respect for his marriage and for Cornelia and her feelings. He knew that someday she might read his diaries.

In Gifford's mind, he already was married, but the books of Emanuel Swedenborg that he and Laura studied explain that one can have a spiritual marriage that lasts for all eternity and a human marriage that is only temporary. If one's true spouse dies, sometimes it is necessary to marry again, but this marriage ends when one dies and is reunited forever with the true husband or wife.

• PISGAH FOREST •

Even before Gifford Pinchot became George Vanderbilt's forester, the Forest Reserve Act of 1891 gave
the president of the United States the right to create
forest reserves from the government's remaining unclaimed
lands, known as the public domain.

In 1897, a year before Pinchot became chief of the Division of Forestry in the US Department of the Interior, Congress passed the Forest Management (or Organic) Act. "The
purpose of the Organic Act was to protect the watersheds of
valuable streams, to maintain the country's forests, to provide
timbered products and to regulate forests for security and fire
protection."[1]

"In 1900, Congress granted $5,000 to the Division of For-
estry and the US Geological Survey to study nearly ten million acres of southern forests."[2] As a result, Vanderbilt invited
government officials to evaluate the area that he called Pisgah Forest to ascertain whether the federal government might
purchase it. In July 1901, Pinchot conducted a ten-day tour
of the mountains of western North Carolina with Secretary
of Agriculture James Wilson, North Carolina state geologist

Professor Joseph Holmes, and the Secretary of the Forestry Association.[3]

Years later, in February 1911, Congressman John W. Weeks of Massachusetts, who had a summer home in the White Mountains of New Hampshire, crafted a bill acceptable to all. "The Weeks Act meant that public forests in the East could now join with western ones in the National Forest System."[4]

Agents with the National Forest Reserve Commission evaluated Pisgah Forest in 1913, but did not approve its purchase. They apparently decided that the forest was already in such good condition that there was no need for the government to protect it. In addition, Vanderbilt's price of six dollars per acre may have been too high.[5]

George Washington Vanderbilt died on March 6, 1914, due to complications following an appendectomy. With the urging of Pinchot, Vanderbilt's widow, Edith, sold 86,000 acres of the property to the US Forest Service for five dollars an acre to fulfill her husband's wishes to create the Pisgah National Forest. She sold additional land as finances demanded in the years that followed.[6]

The Bent Creek Experimental Forest is the oldest federal experimental forest east of the Mississippi River. It encompasses nearly 6,000 acres within the Pisgah National Forest. It was established in 1925 for the purpose of conducting research on silvicultural practices that would aid in the rehabilitation of cutover, abused lands and promote sustainable forestry, and also to provide a field demonstration of forest management practices. Long-term and current research conducted at Bent Creek provides land managers with science-based information and methods to meet their forest management and restoration goals. Demonstration areas and research studies at Bent Creek provide a hands-on way to see the results of different forest management practices and deliver new research findings to land managers, landowners, researchers, students, and the general public.

Today, the spirit of conservation embodied by Gifford Pinchot remains evident in the Pisgah National Forest, not far from the city of Asheville and managed for multiple uses.

· AFTER STRAWBERRY HILL ·

Williiam D. Houghteling died on August 9, 1898, survived by his wife, a daughter, and a son.[1] Marcia Houghteling remained in the Strawberry Hill mansion with a niece until her death on September 1, 1902, after an illness of several weeks.[2]

The Strawberry Hill estate and the Houghteling property in Chicago were listed for sale in 1903. On December 12, 1910, the *Asheville Citizen* ran an interesting story titled "Dr. Winter Opens Strawberry Hill."[3] "Traveling in a private car from Philadelphia and accompanied by her family and servants numbering eighteen persons altogether, Dr. H. Elizabeth Winter, of Philadelphia, arrived in Asheville Saturday to make her home for the winter in this city. It will be recalled that recently Dr. Winter became the owner of the handsome property in West Asheville known as 'Strawberry Hill,' obtaining this at a purchase price of about $13,000. Quite a number of improvements have been made in the handsome house. It is the intention of Dr. Winter to make this her winter home in the future."

Dr. Winter occupied the property for less than three years. Col. P. G. Bowman and his wife, Marguerite, purchased the property from Dr. Winter in June 1914. The Bowmans were

living there on March 3, 1915, when a fire broke out and com-
pletely destroyed the mansion. They were able to escape, with
some injuries.[4] The remaining barn and servants' quarters on
the 12.5-acre Strawberry Hill property were purchased by Dr.
Martin L. Stevens from Col. Bowman's widow and were used
from November 1916 until May 1927 as the Strawberry Hill
Sanatorium. Dr. Stevens is mentioned in *Fashionable Asheville*
as working with Dr. Karl von Ruck. The 1920 census includes a
list of patients residing there.

The Strawberry Hill property was later acquired by Martin A.
Ryerson, a member of the original group of businessmen who
came to West Asheville from Chicago. Ryerson's tract of ninety
acres was sold to J. C. Penland in April 1924. In June 1925, Penland's ninety acres were purchased by the City of Asheville for
$30,000. In May 1927, Dr. Stevens sold the Strawberry Hill prop-
erty of 12.5 acres to the city along with a much smaller piece.
The two Stevens tracts and the Ryerson/Penland tract are what
became known finally as the 114-acre Rhododendron Park.

It was commissioned on March 12, 1931, as Roberts Park, in
honor of the late Asheville mayor, former US Congressman,
and West Asheville resident Gallatin Roberts, who first suggested a park at that location.[5] Located on Brevard Road overlooking the French Broad River, the view from the park included Asheville, the Craggy Mountains, the Swannanoa Gap, and
the Biltmore Estate.

In 1941, the park became an early precursor of the North
Carolina Arboretum when a "Tree School" to include spec-
imens of 150 trees native to the region was dedicated in the
park.[6] Three years earlier, a committee had been set up to create a rhododendron garden there with samples of the many
varieties found throughout the world.[7]

During his years at Biltmore, Pinchot had collected seeds from many parts of the world to be grown for an arboretum that Frederick Law Olmsted had recommended be part of the estate. It was planned not merely to make a botanical collection, but also to show the value of trees as elements both in scenery and in practical forestry.[8] However, Vanderbilt never provided funds to follow through on the plan.

After World War II, Asheville underwent a large expansion. Some of what had been the Strawberry Hill property was swallowed up in the building of the National Guard Armory off Brevard Road and I-240. On March 31, 1967, the city sold 68 acres of what had been Rhododendron Park to Aston Park Hospital for $100,000. It remains today as the Aston Park Health Care Center on Brevard Road.[9]

Along the river, Hominy Creek Park connects with a greenway to Carrier Park, named for Edwin G. Carrier, on the site of his old horse racetrack along the river. Before that, the area was used for a time as an airstrip for small planes and then for drag racing before becoming the current bicycle racetrack.

In recent years, residents have taken an interest in the history of their area, and an active preservation movement has developed. A twelve-acre route for Edwin Carrier's West Asheville and Sulphur Springs Railway along Hominy Creek has been proposed by Friends of Connect Buncombe as part of the Asheville and Buncombe County greenway system. The land borders two-thirds of a mile of the northern side of Hominy Creek and Buttermilk Creek between Sand Hill Road and Hominy Creek Road. Its southern boundary is the creek and its northern boundary follows the back lot lines of the houses along Shelburne Road.

NOTES

Preface

1. Gifford Pinchot. *Breaking New Ground.* New York: Harcourt, Brace and Company, 1947, 137.

2. Harold T. Pinkett. *Gifford Pinchot: Private and Public Forester.* Urbana: University of Illinois Press, 1970.

Asheville Becomes a Tourist Destination

1. Richard Russell. *Robert Henry: A Western Carolina Patriot.* Charleston: History Press, 2013, 103–104.

2. Ibid., 107.

3. George A. Diggs, Jr., *Historical Facts Concerning Buncombe County Government.* 1935.

4. Lou Harshaw. *Asheville: Mountain Majesty.* Fairview, NC: Bright Mountain Books, Inc., 2007, 88–89. "Edward J. Aston: A Life Sketch of a Prominent Ashevillean." *Asheville Daily Citizen,* December 4, 1891.

5. "Dr. Battle Dies, Funeral Sunday." "Dr. Battle Dies, 2 Cities to Pay Last Tributes" *Asheville Citizen-Times,* April 30, 1927.

6. Harshaw. *Asheville: Mountain Majesty*; Richard D. Starnes. *Creating the Land of the Sky.* Tuscaloosa, Alabama: The University of Alabama Press, 2005, 27.

7. Ina Woestemeyer and John J. Van Noppen. *Western North Carolina Since the Civil War.* Boone, North Carolina: Appalachian Consortium Press, 1973, 256–262.

8. David C. Bailey. *Fashionable Asheville*. Booksurge, 2004, 55.

9. Hinton H. Helper, *Western North Carolina: Nature's Trundle-bed, 1886.*; T.H. Lindsey, *Lindsey's Guide Book to Western North Carolina, 1890.*

10. Carole Currie, "Carrier Responsible for Many 'Firsts.'" *Asheville Citizen-Times*, December 15–16, 1983.

11. Lou Harshaw. *Asheville: Mountain Majesty*; Gertrude Ramsey, "Edwin G. Carrier: Tourist Promoter and Builder of Street Railway Here." *Asheville Citizen*, April 3, 1949.

12. "A Quarter of a Million," *Asheville Citizen*, March 31, 1892.

13. Currie, "Carrier Responsible for Many 'Firsts'": "Carrier, A Transplant Yankee, Did Much for Asheville in 1880–1890s." *Asheville Citizen-Times*, July 17, 1960.

14. Ibid.

15. Bill Alexander. *The Biltmore Nursery: A Botanical Legacy*. Natural History Press, 2007, 17.

Gifford Pinchot

1. Char Miller. *Gifford Pinchot and the Making of Modern Environmentalism*. Washington, DC: Island Press, 2001, 67.

2. Gifford Pinchot. *Breaking New Ground*, 1.

3. Miller, *Gifford Pinchot and the Making of Modern Environmentalism*. 83.

4. *Breaking New Ground*, 27.

5. Miller, *Gifford Pinchot and the Making of Modern Environmentalism*, 101.

6. Gifford Pinchot. *The Conservation Diaries of Gifford Pinchot*, Harold K. Steen, ed. Durham, NC: The Forest History Society, 2001, 52.

7. Ibid., 48.

8. Ibid., 52.

9. Gifford Pinchot. *Biltmore Forest: the Property of Mr. George W. Vanderbilt: An Account of Its Treatment, and The Results of the First Year's Work.* Chicago: R.R. Donnelley & Sons Co., 1893, 10–14.

10. Pinkett, 25.

11. *Biltmore Forest*, 57.

Neighbors

1. *Asheville Daily Citizen*, August 9, 1890.

2. Miller, *Gifford Pinchot and the Making of Modern Environmentalism*, 186.

3. "On Strawberry Hill," *The Weekly Citizen*, June 26, 1890, 26.

4. Ibid.

5. Most of the information in this chapter and chapters 4, 5, and 6 were taken from the late James G. Bradley's article "The Mystery of Gifford Pinchot and Laura Houghteling." *Pennsylvania History*, 66, 2. "The Pinchot Family" (Spring 1999), 199–214, unless other sources are indicated or the text is clearly speculation about what might have happened during Gifford and Laura's courtship. My assumption is that Bradley had access to the portions of Gifford's diary that were later hidden or destroyed and to which I would now have no access.

The Pennsylvania History Society now owns the copyright to the article, and its officers have graciously given me permission to copy from all of it. For the sake of easy reading, I have not used quotation marks except when quoting from another source.

6. Pinchot, *Conservation Diary*, 13.

7. Sheila M. Rothman. *Living in the Shadow of Death: Tuberculosis and the Social Experience of Illness in American History*. New York: Basic Books, 1994, 3.

8. James H. Caine. "Today and Yesterday." *The Weekly Citizen*, 1927.

9. Katherine Ott. *Fevered Lives: Tuberculosis in American Culture Since 1870*. Cambridge, MA: Harvard University Press, 1996, 82.

10. Rothman, 4.

11. Ibid., 20.

12. Pinchot, *Breaking New Ground*, 54.

13. Ibid., 31.

14. The caption for a photo in the April 3, 1947, edition of *The Asheville Citizen* of a new ferry operating across the French Broad River mentions that it replaces "a wooden craft which had been operated for approximately 20 years."

15. James H. Caine. "Today and Yesterday."

16. "The Belmont Burned," *Asheville Daily Citizen*, August 25, 1892; "Frantic Mother," *Asheville Citizen*, from the *Weekly State Chronicle*, Raleigh, NC, August 30, 1892, 5.

17. Ibid.

18. Pinchot, *Breaking New Ground*, 70.

19. John Dupuy Eggleston and J. S. McIlwaine. *Asheville and Vicinity: A Handbook of Information*, 1896.

20. Miller, *Gifford Pinchot and the Making of Modern Environmentalism.*
186.

21. Pinchot, *Breaking New Ground, 57.*

22. Pinchot, *Conservation Diary*, 15.

23. Rather than any serious mental disturbance, the melancholy that she mentions may be related to Gifford's lack of challenge in his work at Biltmore, now that the project for the World's Fair had ended. If he had stayed full-time at Biltmore, his future work for Vanderbilt would have been routine, carrying out the plans that had already been made. This led to his establishment of an office in New York as a Consultant Forester, where he could attract new projects to tackle. Pinchot, *Breaking New Ground*, 69.

Consumption Becomes Tuberculosis

1. Sheila M. Rothman. *Living in the Shadow of Death: Tuberculosis and the Social Experience of Illness in American History*, 2.

2. Thomas Goetz. *The Remedy: Robert Koch, Arthur Conan Doyle, and the Quest to Cure Tuberculosis.* New York: Gotham 2014, 3.

3. Thomas Dormandy. *The White Death: A History of Tuberculosis.* New York: New York University Press, 1999. 2.

4. Rothman, 179.

5. Dormandy. *The White Death: A History of Tuberculosis*, 128–131.

6. Ibid., 180.

7. Dormandy, 140.

8. Goetz.

9. Uvistra Naidoo. *New York Times*, May 19, 2016.

Washington, DC

1. Pinchot, *Breaking New Ground*, 69.

2. Pinchot, *Conservation Diaries*, 15.

Transcendent Love

1. *Conservation Diaries*, 16.
2. Miller, *Gifford Pinchot and the Making of Modern Environmentalism*. 183–184.

Spiritualism

1. Thomas R. Wellock. *Preserving the Nation: The Conservation and Environmental Movements 1870–2000*. Wheeling, Illinois, 2007, 35.
2. Ibid.
3. Pinchot. *Conservation Diaries*, 4.
4. Bradley, "The Mystery . . .," 212.
5. www.swedenborg.org/Beliefs.aspx.
6. Roy Stemman. *Spirits and Spirit Worlds*. New York: Doubleday and Company, 1976, 9–10.
7. Ibid., 10.
8. Miller, *Gifford Pinchot and the Making of Modern Environmentalism*, 411.
9. Michael Stanley, ed. *Emanuel Swedenborg: Essential Readings*. Sterling Publishing, 1988, 138.
10. www.britannica.com/topic/spiritualism-religion.
11. Roy Stemman. *Spirits and Spirit Worlds*, 21–22, 97.
12. Larson, *Thunderstruck*. New York: Crown Publishers, 2006.
13. Ann Braude. *Radical Spirits: Spiritualism and Women's Rights in Nineteenth-Century America*. Boston: Beacon Press, 1989, 3.
14. Sandra L. Katz. *Dearest of Geniuses: A Life of Theodate Pope Riddle*. Windsor, Connecticut: Tide-Mark Press, Ltd., 2003, 43.
15. Ibid.
16. Ibid.
17. Braude, *Radical Spirits*, 201.
18. Rothman, *Living in the Shadow of Death*, 24; quoting Edith W. Gregg, *Our First Love: The Letters of Ellen Louisa Tucker to Ralph Waldo Emerson*. Cambridge: Harvard University Press, 1972.
19. Gay Wilson Allen. *Waldo Emerson a Biography*. New York: The Viking Press, 1981, 160.
20. Emerson's courtship of his second wife, Lydia Jackson, was unusual, in that he had met and spoken with Lydia only a few times before he wrote her a

letter asking for her hand in marriage. After their marriage, Emerson changed her name to Lidian.

21. Paula Ivaska Robbins. *The Royal Family of Concord: Samuel, Elizabeth and Rockwood Hoar and Their Friendship with Ralph Waldo Emerson.* Philadelphia: Xlibris, 2003.

22. http://www.mhs.mb.ca/docs/mb_history/25/doyleinwinnipeg.shtml#11.

23. Katz, *Dearest of Geniuses*, 43.

24. Stemman, *Spirits and Spirit Worlds*, 50; Erik Larson, *Thunderstruck*. New York: Crown Publishers, 2006.

25. Katz, 43.

26. Gerald E. Myers. *William James: His Life and Thought.* New Haven, Yale University Press, 1986, 10.

27. Robert D. Richardson. *William James: In the Maelstrom of American Modernism.* New York: Houghton Mifflin Company, 2006, 150.

28. Ibid., 258.

29. Ibid.

30. Ibid., 261; Myers, 10.

31. Ibid., 4.

Gifford's Career after Laura's Death

1. Pinkett, 49.

2. Pinchot, *Conservation Diaries*, 59–60.

3. Pinchot, *Breaking New Ground*, 65.

4. Marci Spencer. *Pisgah National Forest: A History.* Charleston, South Carolina, The History Press, 2014, 37.

5. Ibid., 67.

6. Ibid., 38.

7. Ibid.

8. Pinkett, 30.

9. Ibid., 31–32.

10. Ibid., 44.

11. Samuel P. Hays. *Conservation and the Gospel of Efficiency: The Progressive Conservation Movement 1890–1920.* Cambridge: Harvard University Press, 1959, 29.

12. Pinkett, 49.

13. "Until around 1970, federal land managers remained obsessed with controlling large fires. But during the 1960s, scientific research increasingly demonstrated the positive role fire played in forest ecology. This led in the early 1970s to a radical change in Forest Service policy—to let fires burn when and where appropriate. It began with allowing natural-caused fires to burn in designated wilderness areas." http://www.foresthistory.org/ASPNET/Policy/Fire/Suppression./Suppression.aspx.

14. Pinkett, 51.

15. Pinkett, 86.

16. Pinkett, 41–42.

17. Wellock, *Preserving the Nation: The Conservation and Environmental Movements 1870–2000*, 28.

18. Hays, *Conservation and the Gospel of Efficiency*, 41–42.

19. Pinkett, 49–50.

20. Hays, *Conservation and the Gospel of Efficiency*, 30–31.

The Administration of President Theodore Roosevelt

1. Pinchot, *Conservation Diaries*, 134.

2. Ibid., 133.

3. Doris Kearns Goodwin. *The Bully Pulpit: Theodore Roosevelt, William Howard Taft, and the Golden Age of Journalism*. New York: Simon & Schuster, 2013, 245.

4. Pinkett, 93; the Bent Creek Experimental Station in the Pisgah National Forest is in the oldest federal experimental forest east of the Mississippi, established in 1925 near Asheville, now abutting the North Carolina Arboretum.

5. Hays, *Conservation and the Gospel of Efficiency: The Progressive Conservation Movement 1890–1920*, 19.

6. Pinkett, 68.

7. Goodwin, *The Bully Pulpit*, 317.

8. Ibid., 134.

9. Wellock, *Preserving the Nation*, 3.

The Administration of President William H. Taft

1. Hays, *Conservation and the Gospel of Efficiency*, 147.
2. Hays, 167.
3. Pinchot, *Breaking New Ground*, 392.
4. Hays, 150.
5. Goodwin, *The Bully Pulpit*, 561; Hays, 149.
6. Hays, 156–7.
7. Wellock, 13.
8. Ibid., 14.
9. Pinchot, *Conservation Diaries*, 142.
10. Wellock, 14.
11. Pinchot, *Breaking New Ground*, 419.
12. Goodwin, 605.
13. Goodwin, *Bully Pulpit*, 12.
14. Goodwin, *Bully Pulpit*, 632.
15. Wellock, 13–14; Goodwin, *The Bully Pulpit, 605*.
16. Wellock, 15.
17. Williams, *Gifford Pinchot and the Making of Modern Environmentalism*, 225.

Marriage to Cornelia Bryce

1. Carol Severance, "Cornelia Bryce Pinchot (1881–1960)," Grey Towers National Historic Landmark, Milford, Pennsylvania.
2. Ibid.
3. Ibid.
4. All quotes are from Pinchot, *Conservation Diaries*, 26–29.
5. Ibid.; Miller, *Gifford Pinchot and the Making of Modern Environmentalism*, 180.
6. Ibid.
7. Ibid., 177–181.
8. Pinchot, *Conservation Diaries*, 16.

Pisgah Forest

1. Marci Spencer. *Pisgah National Forest: A History.* Charleston, SC, The History Press, 2014, 66. Another "Organic Act" was passed in 1916, establishing the National Park Service.
2. Ibid., 69.
3. Ibid.
4. Ibid., 71.
5. Ibid., 72–73.
6. Ibid., 74.

After Strawberry Hill

1. *Asheville Daily Citizen*, August 9, 1898.
2. *Asheville Citizen*, September 2, 1902.
3. *Asheville Citizen*, December 12, 1910.
4. "Two Are Hurt As They Jump From Building Doomed by Flames," *The Asheville Citizen*, Thursday, March 4, 1915.
5. *Asheville Citizen*, March 13, 1931.
6. "'Tree School' Project Is Being Set Up in Rhododendron Park," *Asheville Times*, November 14, 1940.
7. "Plans Made to Improve Park in West Asheville," *Asheville Citizen*, September 9, 1938.
8. Pinchot, *Breaking New Ground*, 55.
9. www.ashevillegardens.com.

BIBLIOGRAPHY

Alexander, Bill. *The Biltmore Nursery: A Botanical Legacy.* Natural History Press, 2007.

Allen, Gay Wilson. *Waldo Emerson a Biography.* New York: The Viking Press, 1981.

Bailey, David C. *Fashionable Asheville.* Booksurge, 2004.

Bradley, James G. "The Mystery of Gifford Pinchot and Laura Houghteling." *Pennsylvania History.* 66, 2. "The Pinchot Family." (Spring 1999), 199–214.

Braude, Ann. *Radical Spirits: Spiritualism and Women's Rights in Nineteenth-Century America.* Boston: Beacon Press, 1989.

Diggs, George A. Jr. *Historical Facts Concerning Buncombe County Government.* 1935.

Dormandy, Thomas. *The White Death: A History of Tuberculosis.* New York: New York University Press, 1999.

Eggleston, John Dupuy and J. S. McIlwaine. *Asheville and Vicinity: A Handbook of Information.* 1896.

Goetz, Thomas. *The Remedy: Robert Koch, Arthur Conan Doyle, and the Quest to Cure Tuberculosis.* New York: Gotham, 2014.

Goodwin, Doris Kearns. *The Bully Pulpit: Theodore Roosevelt, William Howard Taft, and the Golden Age of Journalism.* New York: Simon & Schuster, 2013.

Harshaw, Lou. *Asheville: Mountain Majesty.* Fairview, NC: Bright Mountain Books, Inc., 2007.

Hays, Samuel P. *Conservation and the Gospel of Efficiency: The Progressive Conservation Movement 1890–1920.* Cambridge: Harvard University Press, 1959.

Helper, Hinton H. *Western North Carolina: Nature's Trundle-bed, 1886.*

Katz, Sandra L. *Dearest of Geniuses: A Life of Theodate Pope Riddle*. Windsor, Connecticut: Tide-Mark Press, Ltd., 2003.

Larson, Erik. *Thunderstruck*. New York, Crown Publishers, 2006.

Lindsey, T. H. *Lindsey's Guide Book to Western North Carolina, 1890*.

Miller, Char. *Gifford Pinchot and the Making of Modern Environmentalism.* Washington, DC: Island Press, 2001.

Miller, Char and Kevin C. Brown. "Happy Birthday, Gifford Pinchot," *Pittsburgh Post- Gazette*, August 9, 2015.

Ott, Katherine. *Fevered Lives: Tuberculosis in American Culture since 1870*. Cambridge, MA: Harvard University Press, 1996.

Pinchot, Gifford. *Biltmore Forest: The Property of Mr. George W. Vanderbilt: An Account of Its Treatment, and the Results of the First Year's Work*. Chicago: R. R. Donnelley & Sons Co., 1893.

———. *Breaking New Ground*. New York: Harcourt, Brace and Company, 1947.

———. *The Conservation Diaries of Gifford Pinchot*, Harold K. Steen, ed. Durham, NC: The Forest History Society, 2001.

———. *The Fight for Conservation*. New York: Doubleday, 1910.

Pinkett, Harold T. *Gifford Pinchot: Private and Public Forester*. Urbana: University of Illinois Press, 1970.

Richardson, Robert D. *William James: In the Maelstrom of American Modernism*. New York: Houghton Mifflin Company, 2006.

Robbins, Paula Ivaska. *The Royal Family of Concord: Samuel, Elizabeth and Rockwood Hoar and Their Friendship with Ralph Waldo Emerson*. Philadelphia: Xlibris, 2003.

Rothman, Sheila M. *Living in the Shadow of Death: Tuberculosis and the Social Experience of Illness in American History*. New York: Basic Books, 1994.

Russell, Richard. *Robert Henry: A Western Carolina Patriot*. Charleston: History Press, 2013.

Severance, Carol. "Cornelia Bryce Pinchot (1881–1960)," Grey Towers National Historic Landmark, Milford, Pennsylvania.

Spencer, Marci. *Pisgah National Forest: A History*. Charleston, South Carolina, The History Press, 2014.

Stanley, Michael, ed. *Emanuel Swedenborg: Essential Readings*. Sterling Publishing, 1988.

Starnes, Richard D. *Creating the Land of the Sky*. Tuscaloosa, Alabama: The University of Alabama Press, 2005.

Stemman, Roy. *Spirits and Spirit Worlds*. New York: Doubleday and Company, 1976.

Stradley, David, ed. *Conservation in the Progressive Era: Classic Texts.* Seattle: University of Washington Press, 2004.

Wellock, Thomas R. *Preserving the Nation: The Conservation and Environmental Movements 1870–2000.*

Woestemeyer, Ina and John J. Van Noppen. *Western North Carolina Since the Civil War.* Boone, North Carolina: Appalachian Consortium Press, 1973.